Thanks for reading!

Dave Schmoler

"Dave Schmelzer is not the religious type, but his spirituality rings with the kind of authenticity many of us are seeking. Not only that, but he's a delightful writer, evoking the work of Anne Lamott (without the cussing) and Donald Miller."

BRIAN D. McLAREN
Author and activist

"With prose as warm and conversational as an old friend just trying to share some good news, former atheist David Schmelzer does an admirable job here of encouraging us to look at the possibility of a life rooted in the mystical, a life where a faith in Jesus is not restrictive but freeing. As someone who could well be called an unbeliever, I find this book to shine with the kind of non-judgment that might, just might, get me to consider much of what David Schmelzer gracefully argues here."

ANDRE DUBUS III
Author of *House of Sand and Fog*

"I was one of those who didn't see myself as the religious type, who sought the Truth, who wanted life to matter, but who stayed as far away as possible from prepackaged Christianity. . . . Dave encourages us that as long as we're moving toward God, in the best and worst of times, when we don't have all the answers, we will have access to an infinity of good things."

SUE BROWN, PH.D.
Resident dean of freshmen, Harvard College

"Dave Schmelzer provides a new voice that can speak about Jesus to the most hard-boiled secular and academic audiences in the United States. In the combined clarity and sophistication of his message he has become very much an American C. S. Lewis. It is hard to overstate the potential of his work, for in creating a new

Not the

RELIGIOUS

Type

Confessions of a Turncoat Atheist

DAVE SCHMELZER

SALTRIVER®

An Imprint of Tyndale House Publishers, Inc.

CAROL STREAM, ILLINOIS

Visit Tyndale's exciting Web site at www.tyndale.com

TYNDALE and Tyndale's quill logo are registered trademarks of Tyndale House Publishers, Inc.

SaltRiver and the SaltRiver logo are registered trademarks of Tyndale House Publishers, Inc.

Not the Religious Type: Confessions of a Turncoat Atheist

Designed by Ron Kaufmann

Library of Congress Cataloging-in-Publication Data

Schmelzer, Dave.
    Not the religious type : confessions of a turncoat Atheist / Dave Schmelzer.
        p. cm.
    Includes bibliographical references.
    ISBN-13: 978-1-4143-1583-6 (hc)
    ISBN-10: 1-4143-1583-X (hc)
    1. Schmelzer, Dave. 2. Vineyard Christian Fellowship–Clergy–Biography. 3. Evangelists–Biography. I. Title.
BV3785.S27A3 2008
277.3′083092—dc22
[B]   2007048191

Printed in the United States of America

14   13   12   11   10   09   08
 7   6   5   4   3   2   1

For Grace

CONTENTS

Welcome to Final Participation . . . . *ix*

PART I: THE UNIVERSE **1**

If I'd Known This Was Possible, I'd Have Signed Up a Long Time Ago 3

It Turns Out I'm Not Smart Enough to Understand Churches 9

How M. Scott Peck Saved My Life 17

I'm Not a Jerk! (I May, However, Be a Fool) 29

Why—I'm Guessing—You'd Rather Live in Paris than Tehran 37

I'm Better than You (Hang On—That Didn't Come Out Right) 51

PART II: GOD **63**

A Word from Our Lawyers 65

On Second Thought, Disregard Everything I've Said 67

You—Yes, You!—Can Hear God's Voice 77

Nobody Suspects My True Identity 85

Evidently My Options Are either to Be (a) Bored or (b) Terrified 99

How *Baywatch* Caused 9/11 109

I Want Lots and Lots of Sex 121

PART III: HAPPINESS **129**

I Was Pretty Bummed Out Yesterday 131

Sometimes My Prayers Feel Pretty Lame 139

Isn't Faith Always Just One Step from Being Disproved?............147

Three Cheers for Thoughtful Atheism! 151

I Certainly Need All the Help I Can Get............................155

PART IV: WELCOME TO YOUR CENTERED-SET LIFE 161

Some Inside Dirt on Pastors......................................163

If I'd Known This Was Possible, I'd Have Signed Up a

   Long Time Ago 171

Notes *177*

Acknowledgments *178*

About the Author...*180*

Welcome to Final Participation

I got a call a few years back from PBS. They'd heard that I lead a church full of Harvard and MIT and Boston University and Tufts deans and faculty and postdocs (and construction workers and stay-at-home moms and social workers and cooks) who claimed to experience all sorts of miracles and who leaped and rolled around when they got together. This, said PBS, sounded like a story.

I said that everything they had heard was true except for the leaping and rolling around part.

Really? they asked. No leaping and rolling around? But that was the juicy part!

And thus ended our conversation.

I think they missed an opportunity, because the other aspects of the story have some punch on their own. For the last four hundred years, there have been two camps of people in the Western world. First, we have the hardheaded academic types, products of the Enlightenment who scoff at claims of the supernatural. (By and large, these would now include not only those who run our universities but also those who run our newspapers and quite a few who create our entertainment.) And then we have pretty much everyone else, who—at least in theory—is open to the thought that there's more to the world than meets the eye.

My story—as well as many of my friends' stories—
bridges these two worlds. I grew up secular and became
an outspoken debater with religious people. And then I
stumbled upon what seemed suspiciously like a supernatural, active God. But I didn't leave my culture behind,
which made me something of an oddity to friends in both
camps. A secular supernaturalist? What on earth?

Some years ago I read a long, dense essay that gave
some words to what I had gone through.[1] Written by law-
yer and philosopher (and friend of C. S. Lewis and J. R. R.
Tolkien) Owen Barfield, the essay proposed a progression
for all of human history. Humans began with what he called
"original participation." In this first phase, we saw the entire
world as being connected to us, with gods in the sky and in
the bushes. This is the enchanted world that Shakespeare
commented upon in *A Midsummer Night's Dream*.

In the second phase, we pulled ourselves outside of
the rest of the world and became dispassionate observers
of it. You might call this "non-participation." The planets
weren't gods; they were rocks orbiting the sun! Plants
weren't green because of their own whim—we wouldn't
wake up and find that they'd decided on blue. This was the
post-Enlightenment world that Barfield lived in, and that
those of us in the West lived in until only a few decades
ago.

But, Barfield said, human history is heading for a
third and ultimate phase, which he called "final participation." Here the two worlds come together and hardheaded

rationalists will reconnect with a universe that's alive and personal.

It seems to me that's what I'm seeing in Boston. And that this not-quite-articulated hope of final participation is calling to people all around the Western world who thought they were alone—misfits among their skeptical friends and misfits in their churches.

You may have noticed that we're experiencing a renaissance of outspoken, public atheists who forcefully claim that they're the hope of the world and that, if they're ignored, the East and the West will destroy each other. I swim in the sea of these folks—periodically speaking to groups of them—and I think that to a great extent they're right about what they bring to the table.

But not infrequently these critics sound a few troubling notes in print. They often come across—forgive me for being so blunt—as humorless, joyless, and judgmental. They don't seem as if they would be ideal dinner guests, although I'm told that several of them are quite gracious if you get them alone and steer them away from this subject. So how can these writers be right in believing that their unique insight is so crucial and yet come across as so adrift in the bigger picture? These important people will waft in and out of our story to follow.

And let's face it, you may find it to be a strange story, filled with experiences and theories and guileless spiritual tips and the occasional cheerful polemic. But perhaps it makes sense if we see it as belonging to the forgotten genre of confession. You'll recall some famous examples by Augustine and Teresa of Avila and Patrick, who wrote to the authorities of their day to justify their quirks. Their confessions included elements of memoir and spiritual instruction and their spin on history and what they believed were new ways of looking at both the observable world and the hidden world.

Are my friends and I right about all of this? That's a tough one. Yes we are, in the sense that the stories that follow are, best as I can tell, 100 percent true. But more and more, it seems to me that *right* isn't the word we're looking for in talking about such things, that—as we'll talk about—there's actually no possibility of being "right" on these terms.

This idea galls folks on both sides of this conversation. Religious people and skeptics do, after all, agree on one thing: They're very invested in being right. I think my friends would sooner punt to being "on to something" and find that satisfying—maybe even shockingly satisfying—on its own terms.

But this can be an acquired taste. So perhaps you'll need to decide if being on to something is enough for you at this stage of your life. Or perhaps you'll find it to be exactly what you need.

PART I

THE UNIVERSE

If I'd Known This Was Possible, I'd Have Signed Up a Long Time Ago

I'M IN THE MIDDLE OF THE NOVEL *How to Be Good*, by Nick Hornby, and I can't say I'm enjoying it as much as I'd hoped to. It's about a demoralized London doctor and her angry husband, who undergoes a strange conversion and becomes utterly good—selfless, concerned about the wider world, sacrificial. But rather than being comic, as Hornby customarily—and brilliantly—is, he strikes me here as grim. The world he paints offers two choices for our lives: guilt-ridden, culturally savvy liberalism or humorless, scarcity-obsessed goodness. It's as if we can (a) write for the *New Yorker* or (b) lead the Bolshevik Revolution.

Not that this has an entirely unfamiliar feel to me. In my teen atheist years, my mom tried to convince me to go to church because it could offer me "a good thought for the week." She's a great lady, but this didn't do it for me. Like all people, I was already sold on my goodness, if not my happiness. (Al Capone infamously saw himself as a selfless champion of the little people.)

Of the hundreds of people I've seen encounter God over the last few years, one thing nearly all of them have in common is that they never—*never*—saw themselves as the religious type. I live in the shadow of Harvard, where almost no one sees himself or herself as the religious type. (A 1995 survey—hard to pin down but widely quoted—found that only 2 percent of folks living in my city went to church on a given week, compared to 35 to 40 percent nationwide.) But my friends would, almost to a one, tell you that what's happened to them has had very little to do with making them better people, as happy as that thought might be.

For instance, I asked some of them to take a minute and write down what has happened to them on a napkin-sized piece of paper. I got responses like this:

> Me before: No friends, into pornography, broken marriage, horribly burdened at work, couldn't sleep at night, detached from my own emotions, complete lack of hope for the future, favorite saying (no joke): "Every day is worse than the one before."

> Me after: Great friends, incredible hope, sexually pure, conversations with my Creator, sleeping eight hours a night, improved relationship with my ex-wife, have seen my family find God, seeking God's will in my life and knowing he will fulfill it.

Or:

I prayed that I would be healed from anorexia and am now at a healthy weight and have rejoined the track and cross-country teams at my college.

Or:

I found out that my aunt and uncle's marriage was unraveling due to an affair. I fasted and prayed for them. After thirty-eight days, I was contacted by my uncle. He was about to sign a lease on an apartment to move in with his lover. Before he could sign, he felt an almost audible voice in his head say, "stop." He went back to my aunt and started to see how their marriage could be saved. She found a way to forgive him. He was calling me to find out whether this voice was Jesus. It's been about three years and my aunt and uncle are happily together (and my eleven-year-old cousin is doing great). They are both following God now and have since then encouraged me in faith.

When people find out where I live and the types of people I spend my days talking to, they assume that I have a lot of heady conversations about truth and proofs and theorems. But I really don't have heady conversations very often (though I am trying to learn a little more about physics so I can nod at the right place in conversations).

What I *do* talk about again and again is one particularly depressing day I had as an atheist when I spun around to see if there was anything else out there—and seemed to slam straight into a God bent on giving me all sorts of incredible and unexpected things.

I recently was reminded about a Hebrew word—*hesed*—that, when applied to God, gets translated as "mercy" or "kindness" and tells us two things: (1) God will keep his end of the deal, and (2) God will blow us away with shocking acts of kindness, love, and power when we least expect them. My friends and I tell stories along these lines quite a bit.

I've got a lot of problems, trivial and otherwise, as I'll talk about soon enough. So on the mundane side, I used to be thinner than I am now, which feels discouraging. And then there was the day when my baby daughter went from being this vibrant little girl to being—as I was told by the cardiologist who checked her in—maybe the sickest child in a hospital where people bring the sickest kids from all over the world.

And you've probably noticed that the world has a lot of problems. I've spent time in Lebanon, and I have a few friends there. As I write this, Lebanon is being bombed into rubble, and I'm getting e-mails each day about my friends' harrowing attempts to get out of the country alive. You've noticed similarly wrenching items in your morning paper. In the face of problems like this, perhaps the only appropriate response would be a permanently furrowed brow, as if God himself must live a righteously grim life.

And yet there are very few times when, as I'm lying down for the night, I don't think about what's happened to me and shake my head in wonder. How I got to this point has felt like one strange journey.

It Turns Out I'm Not Smart Enough to Understand Churches

BUT BEFORE I GET TO MY JOURNEY, did I mention that, where I live, pretty much no one likes church people or hopes to join them? It would be like aspiring to be a jihadist—clearly that's something that some people want to do . . . but no one I know.

In my neighborhood, it's assumed that church people live far, far away. And while my neighbors are vaguely aware of and unsettled by the looming *threat* of church people—they had a stretch of winning national elections, for instance—for the most part, no one hears from them. Church people aren't making movies or TV shows. They're not writing for the *Times* or any major newsmagazine. They're not winning hoity-toity book awards—or, for that matter, running practically any Western nation.

But perhaps—even here—the times, they are a-changing. I got an e-mail today, for instance, from a local university professor who recently dropped by my church:

> I am writing now because of the idea that you all have a special mission in Cambridge. If you could sense the combination of horror, amusement, and joy that I should find myself accepting the label of someone trying to follow Jesus in any form, you would get a glimpse into the challenges and the rewards of waging a spiritual battle in the most hardened of cynical minds. In a sense we have become anti-Puritans who have purified ourselves of those troublesome spiritual notions that led the first settlers here. But I wonder if that is not just a winter before a new and even warmer spring.

That new and even warmer spring is the subject for this book. And this spring seems to be warming not just the cultural leaders who have—in recent decades, at least—been so cold to faith but also longtime church people looking for a door into the faith they've believed in but perhaps not experienced as much as they had hoped to.

And I don't just *live* in this neighborhood; these are my people! So my first step after leaving atheism as a college student wasn't to head for my neighborhood church but to sign up for courses on Sufi Islam and modern Judaism. My second step was to hit the library and check out books on Hinduism, Taoism, Buddhism, and Confucianism. But, yes, my third step was to concede defeat by canvassing fellow students at dinnertime to find out if any of them went to a church and would be willing to let me tag along.

And so one Sunday I went to my first willingly embarked-upon church service. It turned out to be a "special service" at my new friend's Bible church, a large church in a Spartan building. After singing an opening hymn, we learned that a leader in the church had been having an affair and refused to leave the woman. The hundreds of us in the congregation that morning were encouraged to call the man and urge him to reconsider. But, until then, the pastor wanted us to know that the man was not allowed to return to the church. We sang something and went home.

Was this, I asked my companion, what happened in churches? No, of course not; clearly this was an exceptional service. I should give them another shot. So I went back the next week and heard a forceful argument for why women shouldn't speak in churches, and that was my last week in church for a bit.

This did, however, kick off an eighteen-month period when I gave myself to trying to figure out who this God was that I suddenly seemed to believe in. I quickly realized this search might not be as easy as I'd hoped it would be. I visited a Hindu guru and a Jewish circumcision ceremony. I spent hundreds of hours trying to learn how to pray. I read.

Despite my previous atheism, the problems I encountered with churches weren't new.

When I was a kid, my father was not interested in church, though my mother certainly believed in God and wanted my sister and me to be raised in a church. So we were regulars at a mainline church whose main features, from my seven-year-old vantage point, were children's teachers who hated children. I can still picture them sighing when they discovered that, against all hope, we'd come back that week.

Just after I turned ten, my courageous sister announced she was through with that church. She was strong willed enough that—as I hid behind a chair and silently cheered her on—she won. That was the end of church for us, except for occasional befuddling visits on Easter or Christmas Eve.

In my teens, when I did attend with my mom on those rare occasions, my problem wasn't that I disagreed with what happened there. My problem was that it was gibberish to me, a code other people seemed to understand and nod knowingly in response to but that my foggy brain processed as a mix of theological jargon, obvious moralisms (*surely there must be more to it than I'm understanding*), repellent moralisms (*again, surely there must be more to it than I'm understanding*), and obscure commentary on obscure passages from the Bible.

My atheism (or maybe it was just hard-line agnosticism; the difference is blurring for me these days) hardened in my early high school years in San Diego. Everything seemed absurd to me—certainly everything I was being taught but also everything I had been told about the world. I remember seeing a *60 Minutes* exposé on corrupt preachers, which strengthened my general theme. But I talked with a lot of my churchgoing classmates about why they believed in God and I usually got one of two answers: Their parents believed in God, which was good enough for them, or they had a relationship with God. The first I dismissed, and the second I mocked. A *relationship*? Like they . . . what? Went to the *movies* with God? Took him rock climbing? The few who didn't walk away at that point might tell me that God heard and answered their prayers or that—and this was especially nutty to me—they talked with God and he talked back.

So my point of view gradually took shape. Whether or not there was a God was moot, because we could never have proof. There was no "answered prayer" that could conclusively be proven as supernatural. And whatever comfort these people might get from their chats with God, we could never know that they were connecting with God rather than their own hearts. If there was in fact a God, it was clear to me that an unbridgeable chasm stood between us, so who really cared anyway?

My first week in college I found myself arguing this point with three Christians in the lobby of my freshman dorm. They were good-natured and smart, and the conversation went on for some time. As people heard us, we drew rooting sections, maybe thirty people total. So from the first days of my college career, I was tagged as the dorm atheist.

Which made it especially embarrassing two months later when I began wondering if there was in fact a God.

Looking back, my reasons seem superficial. A professor mocked me in class for something I thought I'd done especially well. Another teacher moved up a deadline on a paper and suddenly I saw with new clarity how close I was to failing the class. And those two things were enough to make me question the whole basis of my life, which at that point might best have been summarized as:

1. Get into a good school.

2. Get good grades.

3. Get a good job.

4. Marry a good woman.

5. Make good money.

6. Die with a good bank account for my beneficiaries to enjoy.

The day's turn of events suddenly put number two at serious risk, and without number two, there *were* no numbers three through six, and where did that leave me? And, now that I was thinking about it, what kind of moronic philosophy of life was this anyway?

And it wasn't as if even this horrible day was the beginning of the bleakness I was feeling. I'd always looked up to artists, particularly writers. The cool artists of the day were all bearded hippie types, so I'd done my best to become that person. It struck me that on rainy days, what with the hood, beard, and glasses that darkened in the sun, I was all but invisible. I'd become that hidden would-be artist, guardedly peering out at the world with cynicism and fear. When I told a friend that great novelists were the people I admired the most, he cut out a newspaper article that surveyed the happiness of fifty great American novelists, pretty much all of whom came out as "near suicidal." It had begun to feel as if I was fast on track to join them—and, sadly, not in their greatness but in their gloom. And now this.

I didn't know who I could talk to about these feelings. I was new enough at school that I didn't yet have close friends, and it seemed too pathetic to call my high school friends or, obviously, my parents.

Then suddenly I wondered: What if the religious people were on to something? I mean, it all struck me as insanity, but at this point the heck with my philosophy (what had it, after all, done for me lately?) and three cheers for any port in a storm! It wasn't even so much that I was hoping for a God who could bail me out of my messes; I was more hoping for a God who would just *talk* with me, as he evidently did for my partners in debate. I was dying for some perspective, for any sense at all that everything was going to be all right.

So I closed all the shades on my windows for fear of being seen. And I prayed for the first time in a long time, along the lines of, *God, I don't believe that you're real. But if I'm wrong, today would be a terrific day to show me.* And that was it. It had remarkably little immediate effect. No lightning. I didn't feel anything different.

I decided to get away from there, to take a drive, maybe see a movie, *leave.* And that decision kicked off the most insane and pivotal night of my life.

How M. Scott Peck Saved My Life

YES, I'M TALKING ABOUT EIGHTIES pop psychology guru M. Scott Peck, he of *The Road Less Traveled* fame, and no, he didn't save my life; that's total hyperbole.

But it feels like he saved my life.

I liked his hit book as much as the next reader, and yes, life is indeed difficult, as he so memorably began the book. But it was an obscure lecture he gave years later that did the lifesaving for me. I read an account of it some years after my encounter with God that had—as we'll continue to explore in the next chapter—spun everything around for me. But one thing hadn't changed: my relationship with churches, which remained challenging. Enter Peck.

You can find the lecture in his book—shamelessly titled to capitalize on his earlier glories—*Further Along the Road*

Less Traveled. In chapter 7, "Spirituality and Human Nature," Peck talks about an odd thing he'd noticed in his practice. Some patients would begin therapy as deeply troubled, deeply religious people. He'd help them, and—to his mind—part of their clear growth would occur when they'd leave their religion behind. Other patients, just as troubled and then just as helped, would *find* faith as a result of their work together. What did that mean?

That question agitated Peck into proposing a four-stage theory of human spiritual and emotional development. He proposed that, in a perfect world, our spiritual development would exactly track with our emotional development. But, given our *actual* world, it rarely works that way. Traumas along the way can stop our growth in an earlier stage, which has implications not only on how we see the world but also in the way we regard other people and the purpose of life.

Peck's first stage—I'll call it the *criminal* stage—corresponds to the toddler years. Toddlers are cute and loving, but in the broader sense, they don't care about *you*. They can't. That's not the stage they're at. As they're throwing a tantrum over a toy they've been denied, toddlers rarely stop themselves to say, "But you know, this isn't the most important thing in the world, and I haven't once asked how *you're* doing, Daddy. Has it been a good day?"

You could make the case that people who get stuck in the criminal stage are often best served by two institutions: jail and the boardroom. Jail for obvious reasons. In stage 1, our lives are chaotic, which can feel horrifying.

Without boundaries (something provided by good parents), we just grab for whatever we can get. Jail is the ultimate boundary, which explains why some criminals can be model prisoners, but when they're released, they go on an immediate crime spree and get thrown—to everyone's relief—back into jail.

But high-functioning stage 1 folks can often be quite effective businesspeople (or politicians or, God forbid, pastors), because they're relentlessly focused on winning, on getting what they want, whatever it takes.

On the spiritual front, these would often be the addicts and criminals, folks who find God after hitting bottom.

We might call stage 2 *rules-based*. This would correspond to age six or seven. Now you care what Mommy and Daddy think, what they want, what the rules are. My oldest son had a memorable transition to stage 2 even as his younger brother was firmly in stage 1. My wife, Grace, and I are occasionally in quite expressive spiritual circles, which means that we've been in worship meetings where folks would, say, prostrate themselves, lift their hands, or even dance. Our oldest would survey the crowd to see whatever the appropriate behavior was and then he'd warily imitate it. Meanwhile, his brother would be taking laps around the room or heading for the stairs to the stage. The oldest would try to maintain whatever pose he'd taken while, through the corner of his mouth, spitting out his brother's name, trying to get him to shape up. Finally we'd say to him, "That's not your job. We're the parents here. We'll take care of it." And he'd shoot us a look to the effect of, "Evidently not very well!" Stage 2.

Two institutions might best serve stage 2: the military and the church. The military, again, for obvious reasons. It has famously been a transitional institution for people coming from chaotic backgrounds. It's where they find discipline and boundaries. But it was the church part that grabbed my attention. Peck argues that most churches are stage 2. They exist to tell people the rules, to set the boundaries of life.

He takes great pains not to judge this. He emphasizes that whatever spiritual things happen at these churches are undoubtedly completely real and that, to his mind, the teachings there are effectively true. The heart and soul of America and most countries are right here in stage 2. These are the good people who get things done and raise strong families. The larger point rests, rather, in how this and other stages interact with each other. So let's go on for a moment.

Stage 3 could be described as *rebellious*. This corresponds to the teen years. At this stage, the healthy kid begins to question the rules she has been taught in stage 2. Why are they the be-all and end-all? What's *behind* these rules? Often the answers the teen gets are not convincing, particularly if the world around her is stage 2. Then she's most likely to hear, "Quit being such a smart aleck!" and not much more. This often hardens the teen into stage 3, and the wars begin between her and all things stage 2.

The institution that seems best to support stage 3 is the university. Periodically we hear cries of alarm from conservative circles that universities are monolithically liberal. And according to Peck's theory, of course that's true and always will be true. Universities are filled with eighteen- to twenty-one-year-olds, who—as a group—are transitioning into stage 3.

Whole societies, at the broadest level, can also reflect these stages. So, stereotypically at least, the Bible Belt might reflect stage 2. And, meaningfully to me, Cambridge, Massachusetts—dominated by universities—would be stage 3 central.

Again, to recap what we have so far:

Stage 1: criminal

Stage 2: rules-based

Stage 3: rebellious

As we said, Peck was most concerned with the way the stages interact with one another. Stage 2 is an important but often embattled stage. On the one hand, in stage 2 religious communities, there's the assumption that anyone outside of the community is stage 1, a lawbreaker who needs to find God—meaning: to *keep the rules of life*. Stage 3 is especially threatening to stage 2, because folks in stage 3 are seen as unique kinds of lawbreakers—they're rebellious *libertines*!

In this way of thinking—forgive me if I'm offending any political sensibilities, and I'll happily hastily backtrack if we ever chat about this—the Republican party would be stage 2 and the Democratic party, although perhaps not intuitively, would be a blend of stage 3 and stage 1.

Stage 2 and stage 3 each heap scorn on the other, but there's a different *feel* to their scorn. The scorn coming from stage 2 toward stage 3 might be reflected in the use of the word *liberal* as a self-evidently shameful thing, as so obviously shameful you don't even have to say *why* it's shameful. And on the other side, if you were to take a drive in my city, you'd see hundreds of anti-Republican bumper stickers that all boil down to how obviously idiotic and beneath contempt stage 2 people are, leading one to wonder if the Republicans are standing in for the stage 2 *parents* of these drivers.

A fascinating and unexpected corollary in Peck's thinking—central to his experiences with his patients that led to the formulation of his theory in the first place—is the observation that stage 3 *is* spiritual advancement from stage 2. And yet there's every possibility that—if you believe in such things—in stage 2 you'll go to heaven and in stage 3 you'll go to hell. As the saying goes, stick *that* in your pipe and smoke it! Peck's theory explains the contempt stage 3 folks often feel toward the stage 2 faith they've left behind, that strange brew that often comes out as something like, "I don't believe in God, but I'm still more spiritually advanced than *you* are."

Now, before going on to Peck's stage 4, it's worth qualifying this for a moment. Stage 3 folks are indeed spiritually advanced in one limited sense, but not in all senses. Let's say a godly, faith-filled, stage 2 seventy-year-old, someone who has given her life to loving God and loving others, was walking through one of Cambridge's many town squares and ended up in a conversation with some snarky, stage 3, nineteen-year-old. Who is more spiritually advanced? Obviously, in any meaningful sense, it's the older, godly woman. But Peck's point is that there is, nonetheless, a sense in which it's the cocky kid. Hold that thought.

What stage 3 people usually don't realize is that there is a stage 4, that there actually *are* answers to the questions they've been asking. You might call this the *mystical* stage. Here, one suddenly realizes that most of the things we were taught in stage 2 are, in fact, true, but in a much richer and more mysterious sense than we would have, or could have, imagined.

So let's take this spiritual truism from the biblical tradition: "Believe in the Lord Jesus and you will be saved." Stage 2 reads this as: Okay, as of today at 3 p.m., I *did* believe in Jesus, so I can take it to the bank that I'm going to heaven, whatever happens. I believe!

Stage 4, on the other hand, might well say: Wow, that's one profound statement. I *think* I believe, but what does *believe* actually mean? Am I believing *now*? What might that look like? And *saved*. Saved in some meaningful sense *now*, or just saved after I die? Paul, after all, says a little later on in the Bible that what matters isn't any outward religious thing we do (circumcision, for instance) but a transformed life, a life that's *being saved*. Is my life being transformed by my belief? (Or perhaps it's not the belief that's transforming me but Jesus himself, in some sort of direct, mystical sense.) Wow! How?

You can see that stage 4 (mystical) is a stage filled with uncertainty to the same degree that stage 2 (rules-based) is, by definition, filled with certainty. Or, to put it differently, stage 4 is about questions; stage 2 is about answers. In this way of thinking, stage 2 looks at truth from the outside, as if it were a book that can and must be mastered. Stage 4 looks at truth from smack-dab in the middle of it, as if truth is everywhere and will take a lifetime just to begin to traverse (which is the joy of it).

Stage 2 folks tend to look at stage 4 folks with profound suspicion: They *seem* to be saying the same stuff, but every word out of their mouths is slippery. Why won't they just "stand on the truth"? What kind of tap-dancing cowards *are* these people?

If there's anything to this theory of Peck's, perhaps you've guessed how it saved my life. I entered faith from stage 3. So when I went to resolutely stage 2 churches, I was baffled. It wasn't that I disagreed with anything they were saying (even though, from what I understood, I often *did* disagree with some of what they were saying); I rather wondered why these things were worth saying at all. The things they talked about struck me as heady, as abstractions that I perhaps didn't have any quarrel with, but I kept waiting for them to tell me something that would call me into the profound but hopeful and life-changing mystery that I seemed to be entering. Instead, I found their whole purpose was to *remove* all mystery, as if mystery were the enemy and certainty were what we were looking for.

Perhaps you'll have guessed, as well, why so many Cambridge folks have found this stage 4 approach to be so significant. Many great people have been commissioned by vibrant, Bible Belt churches to come here and start a new church in the heart of paganism. These churches are often faith filled, but they almost always stay quite small. If Peck is right, stage 2, by definition, cannot reach those in stage 3. Stage 3 people, rightly, are never going back. We often meet folks who grew up in stage 2 churches, who led youth groups there, and who then went to college (that home of stage 3) and lost their faith. When they find their way back with us, what they realize is that—to their surprise—they never quit believing in God. What they quit believing in was stage 2.

Now, perhaps to belabor this point, you might think this would mean that my gang is somehow a lot headier than the average stage 2 church, which just speaks the "plain truth" and not that blah-blah-blah mystery stuff. Strangely enough, it's just the opposite. My friends and I find ourselves telling a lot of stories and very few truisms. In this stage 3 central, this intellectual capital, you'd think we'd be advised not to trumpet things like, say, supernatural healing, but we do. And perhaps some further consideration will help explain that *of course* we do.

Stage 4 is all about life transformation, about a God who actually *does stuff* that we very much want done in our lives, a God who navigates his way through all the evil and pain in the world to somehow triumph in the end, both in our moment-to-moment lives and in the world itself.

For instance, our church periodically attracts flummoxed press coverage—who *are* all these people and how did so many of them end up banding together in such a resoundingly secular city? Here's how we were described by the *Boston Globe* recently (I've changed a name for privacy's sake):

A church takes root in unlikely lefty soil

By Tania Ralli

Globe Correspondent

Last winter, as Janice Chen left her home one day, she slipped on her icy front stairs and her head slammed on a step. Pain shot from her neck to her tailbone. She could barely move.

The next Sunday, with braces on her neck, back, and waist, she was persuaded by her husband to go to church, to get out of the house. . . .

Chen sat through the sermon in pain. Toward the end, a church staff member asked if anyone was in need of prayer. Specifically, he said, someone with a neck injury on his or her right side. "I thought, *What have I got to lose?*" Chen said.

She walked to the back of the room. A member of the church's prayer team placed a hand on her right shoulder and asked God that she be healed. "Within a minute, the pain was gone," she said. "I danced back to my husband, literally." . . .

She says her outlook on life has changed. She's no longer negative or depressed. She feels braver. Most of all, she said, she opened herself to joy.

"If someone had told me a year ago, I would not have believed it," she said.[2]

So. That said. But in the end, the bottom line isn't about this stage-theory stuff, however insightful or helpful it may be. Peck has given many folks I've met the same sigh of relief that he gave me, the perspective on what our spiritual journey has been, what it needs to be, and why we can safely ignore a good deal of well-meaning but inappropriate-for-us spiritual advice. But then, with gratitude, we file all of this until it's next needed.

Because the bigger story is about this unexpected God, this arresting life changer, this profound mystery who is mysterious primarily because of his profound desire to be known, to be walked with, to be drunk into our thirsty spirits, to be lived. That was the God I stumbled smack into on that most pivotal of nights.

I'm Not a Jerk!
(I May, However,
Be a Fool)

AS I'VE MENTIONED, I MEET A LOT of researchers. One day a few years back, I picked the brain of a young neurobiologist who specializes in the study of, of all things, pleasure—something that seems closely tied to what I do for a living. How, for instance, do folks in his field define pleasure? He had a disarmingly simple answer: Pleasure is getting more than you expect. But, he said, that definition leads us to a fundamental problem. Whenever we do, in fact, get more than we expect, our brains adapt to that as a new benchmark, meaning that the same thing won't bring us pleasure the next time. So we go back to the same well, find it dry, try it again just to be sure, and before we know it we're an addict. This even has a fancy name in his trade: the "hedonic treadmill."

The hedonic treadmill has applications for me in endless ways. For one, my gang does try to pleasantly surprise folks who join us. We might ask a dazzling music school student to belt out some current pop tune, which we'll then weave into the theme of the morning. Don't tell me you saw *that* one coming! But we don't have an infinite bag of tricks, which means that the next pop song or scene from Tennessee Williams won't have the kick of the first one. It is—to quote Yul Brynner's character from *The King and I*—a puzzlement.

But here's a strange encouragement along those lines: Evidently, God can bust through the hedonic treadmill. Our team of smart artists and thinkers might not be able to pull it off, but God is on the case.

King David talked about God showing him pleasures that never fade. Jeremiah talked about an experience of life from God that's "new every morning." Paul talked about a God who's eager to do more for us than we can "ask or imagine." And maybe most notably, Jesus said he came to earth for the express purpose of giving us not just rich life but a kind of overflowing life that surprises us, that we couldn't have seen coming. It goes back to this idea of hesed, God's shocking generosity toward us, which—who knew?—turns out to be one of the Bible's central themes.

And that unaccountable generosity was central in what happened to me as I fled my depressing campus. Which, I suppose, might be why it has taken center stage in what has happened to me since.

As I drove away, I thought I'd catch a movie and forget my academic and existential troubles.

After the movie, I popped in a tape that my Taoist sister had sent me a few months back. Someone at her college had invited her to a Christian retreat and my sister had liked it. When she sent me the tapes, I had thanked her but said that I didn't plan to listen to them. And now here I was, not only listening to them but—freaking me out—liking what I heard. Here was someone who spoke in actual sentences and not in code, someone who was openly trying to persuade me of the value of learning about and following the teachings of Jesus. I was free to agree or disagree with him, but at least I'd be forming an opinion about *something.*

After the movie, I found myself disoriented as I drove back to campus. So I took a right, only to discover an equally disorienting, deserted road.

I pulled out an area map, turned on my dome light, held the map over the wheel, and kept driving slowly down the lonely road. Checking the cross streets as I went by, I didn't notice that the road was about to fork and I was about to go straight.

I knocked into a post. Catching my breath, I quickly assessed the damage. I'd been going slowly, so almost certainly the car was fine. (I had an early-eighties Volvo, which had bumpers the size of small states. I was more worried for the post.) And then, as I slowly backed away, I realized that what I'd hit wasn't a post. Filling my windshield was a giant, floodlit cross. It was a church that was on this hill.

Normally this wouldn't have been a big deal, but I had, in fact, prayed *that day* that if there was a God, he'd show himself to me. And now that I thought about it, how many *other* crosses had I rammed?

As my taped conference speaker continued to nudge me toward God, I tried to figure out where I was and how to get back to campus. I took a left, saw that yet again I was on a road that clearly wasn't going to get me home, and pulled into a lit parking lot to again check my map. As I pulled out, something odd struck me: I had parked right underneath a giant, floodlit cross. It was a church parking lot. So that was two giant, floodlit crosses in about a ten-minute span.

Right then I had what I would call a strong impression. I didn't exactly hear anything, but I very much sensed something, which I can quote to this day: *Dave, you always thought that if there was a God, the good news would be that he cares about humanity. I'm here to tell you that there is a God, and I care about you.* End communication.

You can imagine how that went down with an atheist whose argument was that even on the unlikely chance there was a God, the question was still moot, since he is way up there and we are way down here and there is no chitchat between us.

After finally getting home, still suitably freaked out, I didn't tell anyone. But I did decide to keep experimenting with this thing that had gotten me into whatever I'd gotten into—prayer. Just about every night, I took a half-hour walk and I prayed. The goal was to figure out if there really was someone up there. After three months of this, I was sold. A young woman on my hall was a serious Catholic, so I told her my story and asked what she thought of it. She said, "Here's my interpretation. You're a Christian."

I responded that I'd thought she'd say that but I didn't buy it. What I bought was that I was a *theist*—I believed there was something out there. But why that something should have anything to do with Christianity struck me as a non sequitur. I mean, yes, churches and crosses had been involved, but what were the odds of my ramming a mosque in that neighborhood?

So I began my season of comparative religions, of classes and books and church visits. It took about a year and a half of fairly diligent work before I could say—to my satisfaction, at least—that the only persuasive explanation for what had happened to me was Jesus (which, perhaps, was not the same as Christianity, as we'll talk about in the next chapter).

I would love to walk you through what persuaded me. But none of this is meant to be a serious discussion of any world religion—Christianity included. It's not meant to discount vibrant spiritual experience of any of these traditions, but just to share what happened to me.

The key issue in my experience, it gradually began to occur to me, was this idea of a God who takes a personal interest in us to the point of telling us so. This, again, had been both my primary objection to faith and my direct way into it. As I fumblingly continued to pray, I continued to sense that there truly was a God out there who had an interest in getting my attention.

Could this happen, say, in Buddhism? Best as I could discover, the answer on this front was no. I've met some great Buddhists and have enjoyed learning about the teachings of, for one, the Dalai Lama. But thoughtful people have encouraged me that the idea of an actual God specifically trying to say specific things to me wouldn't fit well into a religion that's by and large atheistic. Buddhism would encourage different benefits.

Confucianism? This seemed unlikely, since Confucianism is more a system of wisdom and ethics than a religion per se.

Taoism? As in my sister's experience, the yin and yang had many things to offer, but a personal and ongoing communication with God didn't seem to be one of them.

Hinduism? This call was a bit tougher to make because Hinduism has so many different streams, and some of them do have a mystical component. But I couldn't find any examples of the kind of chatty, ongoing specificity I was falteringly finding.

Which left me with the three "religions of the book"— Judaism, Christianity, and Islam. So I took a university course in Sufi Islam—the Sufis being Islam's mystics. But what became clear to me was that Sufis were rare in modern Islam. Could what was happening to me also happen to the rank-and-file Muslim? Unlikely, if only because Muhammad was considered to be God's final prophet, and my experiences might edge uncomfortably into that territory.

How about Judaism? I didn't run across any modern Jews who talked about hearing God's voice so personally and specifically, although that didn't rule out the possibility, as anyone who has read the Hebrew Bible (or Old Testament) could tell you. But my experience would be considered historic.

And then I got to the New Testament, fairly quickly hitting the book called Acts of the Apostles. And then there it was in chapter 2. After Jesus ascended to heaven, we're told he sent his Holy Spirit to everyone who had faith in him. And here's what happened as a result: All these folks, young and old, could expect to hear God talking to them. This is what devout Jews had been waiting for for centuries, and here it was.

[Insert stunned pause.]

All along, I had assumed that faith systems boiled down to moral codes, or in Hornby's words, "how to be good." All along I had heard that I was some kind of jerk for not following God. Now it seemed that I could breathe easy on that front.

I wasn't a jerk! (On *these* terms, at least.) Sadly, however, it appeared that I *was* a fool. Because a lot more was being offered to me than I was taking advantage of.

Why—I'm Guessing—You'd Rather Live in Paris than Tehran

I HAVE A LOVE-HATE RELATIONSHIP with some prominent atheists.

Now I don't kid myself—I know that most of the most vocal atheists have only a "hate" relationship with me. I believe in God, which puts me on the outs on its own merits, never mind the irredeemable Jesus thing.

But much as I can, on occasion, be annoyed by proudly secular places like most Western European nations, I would still vastly rather live there than I would in Tehran—or, say, Calvin's Geneva, where stray thoughts could get you executed.

Why is it that I'm just as horrified by all the religious awfulness in the world as the secularists are? This was a considerable barrier to finding my way into whatever faith experience I was stumbling into.

I have a six-word theory that has gotten me past this: God is good. Religion is bad.

If you've enjoyed and been helped by a terrific faith community, my theory might raise your hackles, as it should. And I'm all for banding together with spiritually like-minded people. By all means, don't do this alone! But, on the other hand, I'm banking on the hope that if you've enjoyed our conversation to this point, you'll like this theory before we're done and that, if you dig a little, you already agree with me.

Now the theory, of course, only works if "religion" is its own entity apart from God, something that incorporates one's culture and nationalism and judgmentalism and inferiority into some spiritual realities that whip it up into a nice meringue.

This idea seems connected to our conversation about spiritual stages—as well as being surprisingly freeing in our desire to experience hesed, this shockingly good God. What if, for instance, we can separate our growing experience of this God—at least at first blush—from the way we vote or whom we have to oppose? Is it possible to marvel more and more at the great deal we're getting with God and also read the most scathing book from the nastiest atheist and effectively agree with everything he or she says, apart from the conclusions? (And perhaps also apart from the *tone*, which—in the case of the "nastiest" atheist writers, at least—does tend toward arrogance and sanctimony. I mean, do these authors seem happy to you? Is that worth noting?

And now that we're on this subject, is it fair to wonder if a few of these writers project at least a hint of racism and classism? Everyone except educated, white, Western atheists is characterized as a contemptible, dangerous idiot who should—in the view of one popular writer—be legally silenced. Should we take note of that? And most don't seem to have much room in their world for wonder or art, both of which are important to me. And yet they *do* clearly have a key . . . okay, maybe I should just put a whole chapter together on this stuff. Duly noted.)

Some of my friends tell me that they now regard the great religions of the world as *cultures* every bit as much as faith systems and that this insight has helped them quite a bit. For instance, we all know plenty of Lutherans or Jews or Catholics or Muslims who don't practice their faith but also don't cut themselves off from their heritage.

On the other hand, I'm told that in Calcutta alone, there are over a million "Hindus who follow Jesus." But these people are rejected by local Christians because if they wanted to follow Jesus, they ought to be willing to join in with Christianity, whatever the social costs in terms of their culture or caste. But they're not rejected by local Hindus because they've stayed in the culture.

Having spent a little time in the Middle East, I'm friends with a handful of "Muslims who follow Jesus" who have by no means left the Muslim culture for a Christian one. (You'll recall that in Lebanon, for example, Christians and Muslims spent a decade or so killing each other.)

In that sense I suppose I could be called a secularist who follows Jesus since my background was secular/atheist and to this day that feels like my world. I'm baffled at the thought of "Christian fiction" rather than just fiction. Christian pop music is alien to me. Even the idea of the United States being a Christian nation is challenging for me, since my whole experience and upbringing seemed to have been in a secular nation. But my friends who grew up in Christianity by and large see a different America. That's what cultures do. In my mind, this is a big deal.

A while back, a man asked to meet with me in my church office. He had grown up Jewish, which was very important to him. "I was born a Jew, and I'll die a Jew!" was his opening statement. His girlfriend at the time had dragged him to our church. She'd started coming when she decided to revisit the faith of her youth, and it had affected her to the point that she said she wouldn't sleep with him anymore unless he agreed to come once (a powerful strategy, I think you'll agree). In exasperation, he did visit. But then he kept returning on his own, which scared him.

I asked why he kept coming back, and he said before he started coming to our church, he had a huge anger problem, to the point that he'd go out some nights just to find a fight. He'd actually been straitjacketed not that long before. But since he'd been with us and had taken some suggestions he had heard, his anger problem seemed to be gone, which felt miraculous. So now his question to me was this: Was I going to try to make him a Christian if he stuck around? Because just in case I'd missed it, he'd die first.

I told him that I didn't care if he ever became a Christian and that I, of all people, actually had very little investment in Christianity. After a pause, he asked if this was some sort of strange tactic. I said I thought I meant what I'd said, but I had a question for him. Was it all right if I regarded the good things that had been happening to him as because of Jesus? *He* didn't have to think so—that was his business—but was it all right with him if I believed it? I told him that my suggestions about anger had actually all come from things Jesus said to do, and that if we did them, we would get certain results—results that he was in fact experiencing.

The next time I saw him, I asked how he was doing. "I give all praise to my Lord and Savior Jesus Christ, Dave!" he said. Now, for one, this is not a line I would have suggested to him. (Go back to Peck's stage theory for why that's so—and also, perhaps, for why that line was so helpful to *him*.) After a bit of a pause, I said, "Something's happened since I last saw you, hasn't it?"

Indeed something had. His life had come crashing down on him. He decided to leave his girlfriend, for her sake, given his evidently uncontrollable anger. To calm himself, he had taken a cold shower and, in the middle of it, shouted, "Are you *there*, Jesus? Because I could use some help!" And right then, he got hit with something so hard he had to grab the sides of the shower to stay standing. In my world, we would call that "being filled with the Holy Spirit." But whatever you call it, it stunned him and broke his unstable mood right off of him. And now here we were, having the conversation we were having.

God—it turns out—is good! But religion turns out to have much less to offer, being so closely tied to whatever culture we find ourselves in. Paul argued that Jesus came to earth and broke down the "dividing walls" between people. In my experience, Jesus keeps that deal to this day; he's very invested in that deal. Religion, on the other hand, tends to do the opposite.

On this note: What if truth is fundamentally relational? This sounds nutty to anyone who's spent any time in, say, a school. We've spent our lives learning that truth is *propositional* or *abstract*. Truth comes from theorems, from pure logic. Truth is the opposite of emotion, and relationships are emotional.

But that point of view seems to be fraying. Quantum physics, for instance, has pitched that the only way we can know anything is by understanding our own vantage point—meaning that we're in relationship with anything we're trying to prove.

Jesus famously said, "I am . . . the truth," which is a very different statement from "I *teach* the truth." Truth here gets personalized. My reorienting experience in Acts 2 pushed me in this direction: This God is different than others because he wants to talk with and listen to me. In fact, folks who read the Bible are confronted by a God who claims to *be* a relationship—Father, Son, and Spirit.

As someone who loves to read and think new, deep abstractions, I nonetheless find myself wondering if the only things that actually matter are relational—if the Beatles had it right that all we need is love.

In this way of thinking, religion (which, again, is so closely tied to our culture) is usually about rules and codes, about ways to behave, about nonrelational morality (about "being good," whether or not you ever meet another person), about what will get you embraced and what will get you shunned. God, on the other hand, is all about how you can become a closer friend with him, with others, and with yourself. C. S. Lewis pitched a view of hell as a giant, ever-expanding subdivision where—because of continual, petty quarrels—you're ever-increasingly alone.

Let me take you back to math class for a minute and talk about two different kinds of sets. Bounded sets are best pictured as circles. The issue with bounded sets is whether you're inside of them or not. We all have bounded sets. For instance, I'm a man. If you're a woman, sorry, you're on the outside of that one. I'm an American. I'm more than six feet tall. I go to church. And so on. The more we specify our bounded sets, the more we'll ultimately create a set with only ourselves inside of it. Bounded sets.

Centered sets are best pictured as dots. The issue with a centered set involves motion, not whether we're inside or outside. Imagine a dot in the center of your set—for grins, let's call this dot "Jesus" or "God"— and imagine a lot of *other* dots on your page. Let's call those dots "everyone on earth." The issue in each case is whether a given dot is moving toward the center or not.

Let's say I'm really close to the center dot—who, again for our purposes here, we're calling "Jesus" or "God." I'm maybe a foot and a half away. And let's imagine a dot that's a mile away. Way, way off the page. Can't even see that dot with the naked eye, but it's there. And let's say we're both, from our different vantage points, moving toward the center dot. On this theory, we're both doing great. I, of course, have some perks by being so close, but on the most fundamental questions, we're both actually in the same boat. Now let's say that distant dot is, as before, moving in a nice steady line toward the center but I, although much closer, have actually begun to veer a bit. Nothing dramatic, but I've spun away from the center just a skosh. On this theory, that dot a mile away is better off than I am, at least for the moment.

Bounded sets—the circles in this analogy—are religions or cultures. With a religion or culture, you're either inside it or outside it. No gray area here. Now many religions or cultures are benevolent toward those on the outside. They might say something to the effect of, "Hey you outsider. Why don't you jump into our bounded set? It's awesome in here! And, as the *godly* religion/culture, you'll get the chance to be much closer to God than you are at the moment. Yes, there may be a trifling cultural thing or two you'll need to do to accommodate to us, the godly religion/culture. Being a good Illinois Baptist is, after all, a little different than being a good Bengali Muslim, who are we kidding? But we'd love to have you!"

The thing is: Most people don't want a new bounded set. They like theirs just fine. They've spent years getting to know it; they're comfortable with it. And for the most part, bounded sets tend to preach to the choir rather than to outsiders.

Think about this in political terms for a moment. Let's say you're the sort of person who reads the *New York Times* editorial page. Pretty much every correspondent there loathes conservatives and wonders who these idiots are. One of my favorite *Boston Globe* editorial page moments (the *Globe* is a subsidiary of the *Times*) came a few years back in response to one of many editorials ripping George W. Bush, particularly viciously in this case. The next day the paper printed three or four letters, *all* of which had a common point: You, the editorial writers of the *Globe*, are horrible, awful people! Why? Because you didn't rip into Mr. Bush nearly enough! You call that *ripping* him? You should be ashamed of yourselves!

Now let's say you're a conservative reader from a conservative family who stumbles upon this editorial page. What are the odds that you'll read one of these contemptuously anticonservative editorials and think to yourself, *Oh my gosh! They're right! I'm an utter fool (and, goodness, a bigot, to boot)! Who knew? And it's not only me! My family and everyone I've ever known and loved are fools and bigots! Thank you,* Globe *editorial page, for opening my eyes!*

Or let's say you're a committed Eastern liberal who turns on any one of a hundred conservative talk radio programs. What are the odds that you'll experience that conversion in reverse?

The point: Bounded sets preach to other true believers, for the most part. They tend to preach over and against those infidels who aren't a part of their bounded set. And bounded sets often throw a fair number of nonessentials into what it means to be in their set. It's not that these non-essentials might not be reasonable inferences from what's at their center. It's just that a lot of those reasonable inferences accumulate until they're one big ball.

So—taking this from the religious side of things in this instance—let's say you're a part of a church that thinks, as mine does, that following Jesus is a big, big deal. Beyond that, though, let's say most of your friends are antiabortion (something that—as you see it—seems to have plenty of support in the Bible). And maybe it's important to support political candidates who are transparently conservative believers. And when you look around, most of your friends think lobbying for the politics of Israel is a good idea. And you've also got your opinions about things like gay marriage and any wars that might be being fought at the moment. And you have a number of other opinions that strike you as reasonable inferences from believing in Jesus (gender roles, other religions, the role of public schools, good versus bad science, the merits of other churches, church/state separation, maybe even how to dress). Suddenly your bounded set has quite a bit in it, and jumping into it requires a pretty complex maneuver.

That said, let me double back and say: *Bounded sets are awesome!* They do a lot of things right, which is why we all—religious or secular—belong to them. Bounded sets are comfortable because we know the rules and we know what to expect from people. Outside of bounded sets, we often feel on edge; we're outside of our home country.

And yet.

Inside our bounded sets, we do tend to get into shooting wars with outsiders. Of course, you're welcome to *join* our bounded set on our terms, but if, inexplicably, you decline, well, that can only mean you're siding with the bad guys. Nobody's happy that you've made that strange choice. But someone's got to fight for all that's good about our country and world.

Which goes back to why I'd rather live in Paris than Tehran. A defiantly secular culture has its own bounded set, but—if only because I grew up secular—I'd rather live there than in a defiantly religious one. I don't believe I'd find living under Sharia law to be a freeing experience. In this sense, I do think it's reasonable to blame religion for a lot of the world's ills and, frankly, for being no fun.

And hang on—maybe that gets me back to my atheists. What I appreciate about them is their broadside against religion, which I regard as so timely and needed that I'll devote a whole chapter to this point later in the book. But then before we're done, we discover that—bummer!—*they're* religious, deeply religious. By and large, they hate and oppose all who are outside of their set (most of the world, as a matter of fact, which is always true of bounded sets). They're filled with judgment toward outsiders, whom, for all their invective, they seem to know remarkably little about. Some of them would like to bring in legislation to stop the evil inroads of their enemies. They're certain they're right. And like all who are rigidly locked into bounded sets, they seem to experience little joy. Upon reflection, while I'd like to steer clear of living under Sharia law, I'm pretty sure I wouldn't be any happier under Khrushchev's atheistic state.

The Jewish man in my office would not have responded to any religion I offered, and most certainly not to the complex bounded set that is the Christian religion. *God*, however, was a totally different thing—even if I called that God *Jesus*, a name he never would have imagined he could accept.

But when he started crying out to Jesus—"crying out" to Jesus as a *relational* choice rather than the abstract "considering truth claims" about Jesus, and crying out to *Jesus* rather than to *Christianity*—Jesus seemed quick to reach out to him, and everything changed.

Now my friends who've stumbled into the world of this hesed-flinging God *do* discover that they can't keep this experience alive without banding together with others on this same journey. I do, as you've noted, pastor a church. But I wonder if it might be worth a little thought about how one can walk this journey of faith with others while at the same time taking a shot at maximizing our centeredness and minimizing our boundedness. And you're on to something if you're thinking that this might have some crossover with the stage theory we talked about.

But back up; what about all those inferences that many of us indiscriminately dump into our bounded sets? Are none of them important? Do I refrain from having opinions about those inferences? Absolutely not! I have my opinions and I like them just fine and if you were as enlightened as I am you'd share each and every one.

But along with the writers of the New Testament, I do my best to keep my eye on the center dot, move toward him, and encourage as many folks as I can to recalibrate (one take on the literal meaning of *repent*, for what it's worth) their journeys his way as well. This recalibrating takes a little work. But what we find as we do that is just stunning—encouraging beyond what we could have imagined.

I'm Better than You (Hang On—That Didn't Come Out Right)

YEARS AGO I SAW A TERRIFIC SKETCH about a Cockney laborer who shows up in heaven, surveys it, and calls it "flippin' marvelous." I believe it is, because we see so much evidence for that right here. Take a few more of my napkin stories, for instance.

I asked God to give my brother (who was unemployed for two years) a job and for my parents/ family to find some kind of happiness after a terrible car accident that happened in 2003. After six weeks of prayer, in the same week my brother got a job, I got a job, and my parents bought a new house—a sign from God that, despite trials and tribulations, he still has enormous blessings awaiting us.

I prayed that my college loans would be completely erased, and I got a stamped letter with all my loans returned. The stamp said, "Paid in Full."

My dear husband has been in excruciating pain for twenty years, sometimes passing out from the pain. He has not been able to ride in the car for more than a few minutes at a time. He has not been up to visiting with our friends or having people over. He received prayer on Sunday. During the prayer, I noticed that his back changed from being twisted to straight and his right hip, which had always been higher and more forward than the left, became level. On Monday, without thinking, he leaned over and picked up something off the floor and later tied his shoes for the first time in twenty years. He rode in the car for an hour and a half and did great.

My life has never been better. I have never been this happy and content before.

And my own story is right along these lines. Within a few months of my experience with the crosses on the road, I realized I wasn't anxious anymore, which felt like a whole new mode of being. I shaved the beard and quit wearing the hood. This increasingly communicative God started directing me toward fresh life choices and ultimately toward the woman—hitherto unnoticed by me, her stunning beauty notwithstanding—I might consider marrying. All the dreams I thought I'd have to jettison in the name of practicality were suddenly not only back on the table but seemingly encouraged, as if I had no idea how vast an adventure I had just stumbled into and how central the heart of my passions would become as I took my role in that adventure. My fundamental isolation was swamped by a sea of friends.

I seem to stumble into a procession of crazy experiences like this one that just happened: I prayed for a woman recently who had a decade's history of debilitating fibromyalgia—to the point that each day her husband had to help her get dressed to go to work. The next time I saw her, she told me that she's been healed (as her husband nodded vigorously). All symptoms are gone. After a decade.

Now there's all the hard stuff and discouragements and personal failures too, and those will play a healthy role in the rest of our narrative. But goodness gracious, in the big picture, what on earth *happened* to me? When compared to my starting point, it's as if I've been hit by a bus that knocked me into Oz.

It might be worth a comment about stories like this and others I tell in this book. Can I prove that these stories actually go back to an active God making actual choices on our behalf? That's a question that would have been central to me in my teen years, but these days I have three responses. First, these stories seem real and encouraging enough to the people *themselves*. I mean, whatever we think of the stories, the people are obviously not *lying*. So are we in a better position than they are to judge whether God had anything to do with their experiences? Second, in my world I meet a lot of people turning to God for real help and getting that help. I can't help but see causality. And third, I think of a comment by that wisest of journalists, G. K. Chesterton, who said a century or so ago:

Somehow or other an extraordinary idea has arisen
that the disbelievers in miracles consider them coldly
and fairly, while believers in miracles accept them
only in connection with some dogma. The fact is quite
the other way. The believers in miracles accept them
(rightly or wrongly) because they have evidence for
them. The disbelievers in miracles deny them (rightly or
wrongly) because they have a doctrine against them.[3]

Sounds persuasive to me.

And, in keeping with the last chapter, it seems to me
that any of us who want to experience, again and again, the
kind of God who does such things for us has a fundamental
choice to make. Namely, which do we want more: God or
moral superiority? This is such an unexpectedly central
choice that, to my mind, it deserves some space all to itself.

Living in our bounded sets, we want moral superiority.
We want to sneer. We want to oppose. But we find that those
are their own rewards; we rarely, for instance, find ourselves simultaneously joyful and superior. Humility seems
more the virtue of choice when we encounter a living God.
This really is a land that only the meek can possess.

But shunning moral superiority isn't as easy as it looks.
For instance, Boston sports fans—of which I am one—are
notoriously moralistic, and it's hard not to stand with them.
A Red Sox outfielder of a few years back, for instance, beat
his wife and was booed out of town shortly thereafter. Wife
beating reared its head again a few years later with a visiting
basketball star. His team came to town in a play-off series

shortly after the incident, and every time he touched the ball, he was serenaded with chants of "Wife beater!" Now it's worth saying that I'm proudly in the anti-wife-beating camp. No equivocation there. Down with wife beating! But there was something particularly chilling and joyless in our relentless condemnation of the sinner in front of us.

Is God himself a moralist? On the one hand, of course! What kind of stupid question is that? Isn't there something somewhere about a "final judgment"? Isn't there this thick legal code in the early parts of the Bible, a famous list of ten moralisms, not to mention a huge tradition of disapproving church people? And yet Jesus commands us not to judge anyone, and when his disciples came to him tattling on the misdeeds of others, he rebuked the *disciples* rather than the alleged wrongdoers. Paul said he judged no one, not even himself, which can come across as a scandalous shirking of personal responsibility to us churchgoers.

And I can't help but note the robust heritage of ecclesiastical moralists who crash and burn. We've recently had a high-profile example of this as a famous pastor resigned in disgrace, amid a sea of mocking editorial cartoons. Right or wrong, this story hit me in the gut because I like the guy. If someone in my profession is going to bring public shame on himself, I prefer to sneer at him myself, but that's hard in this case where the man in question has so many terrific qualities, has taught me so much, and has done so much good. But the man has also been an unyielding moralist, which proved to be a problem when it turned out he was deeply embedded in some of the activities he most loudly condemned.

I meet plenty of people who, as was true in my case, want God if he's out there to be found. But I never meet anybody who wants religion. Or who wants *right belief*, as if they're walking around banging their foreheads in fear that maybe they're believing the wrong things. Or someone who wants to finally *be a good person*, as opposed to the evil-hearted conniver he or she has been.

The center of the set, the ball we need to keep our eyes on if we want this sort of life and encouragement, is God. The false leads that relentlessly call to us are moral superiority or confidence that we know the truth, that we believe correctly. Those offer us tasteless broth. The banquet is in a different part of the hotel.

Perhaps you'll remember earlier in this book where I talked about "a new and even warmer spring," a spring that I've found is helping both longtime secularists who never imagined they would become people of faith and also longtime churchgoers who perhaps haven't experienced all from their churchgoing that they had hoped to.

One word for that spring is *joy*. Another is *delight*. Joy, it seems to me, is fundamentally a call to stage 4. Stage 2, in its most hardened state, at least, is not joyful but rather oppositional. Or, perhaps more positively stated, resolute. The godly person there is standing against the demonic onslaught of the culture around him or her.

And stage 3, in its purest form, at least, is also removed from joy. The other day I saw a young man in a café reading a magazine called *Skeptic*. This sounded to me a neat summary of stage 3, along with a statement of its limitations, all in a mere word. Skepticism is, of course, crucial for a growing and responsible life. We do have to *think* just a little bit to find out what's really going on around us. And we'd be wise to take the words of even our preferred opinion leaders with a grain of salt. (As a weekly public speaker, I think my regular listeners would be well served by that advice.) But skepticism is not a worldview in and of itself. Adopting a posture of disbelief doesn't get us anywhere, and identifying ourselves primarily as skeptical just seems wearying and downbeat. But we do know who the bad guys are, and there's comfort in that.

But if you were to split the atom of stage 4, in the middle of all of its sorrows and challenges, you'd find joy. It's the bottom line, the irreducible element. And it's a gift whose power becomes especially clear when nothing else offers any comfort.

My wife, Grace, and I learned this when our daughter was horribly ill. When she was about four months old, she developed nursing problems and the doctors gave her the label "failure to thrive." We couldn't get her to eat more and she began to lose weight. By the time she was six months old, we were taking her to the doctor every other day or so, trying to find out what was wrong.

And then one Saturday, Grace was trying to convince her to nurse when the baby's eyes began to dilate and undilate, back and forth. Grace rushed her to the doctor yet again, and she was immediately raced to the cardiac unit of a top children's hospital in the area. I stayed at home with our other kids, and I vividly remember the first thing our cardiologist said when she called me: "I think if everything goes right, there's a chance she'll live." A chance she'll *live*? I'd thought we were talking about a few problems nursing!

It turned out our baby had a rare heart defect that had been missed at all her screenings. Her coronary artery was in the wrong place so it wasn't pumping oxygenated blood back into her heart. Her heart had been dying for months, and now it was pretty much useless. The doctors planned to try a very delicate surgery. If it took, there was still a chance her heart could recover. If not, she would need a transplant, and that was a bleak prospect, because there just aren't a lot of baby heart donors.

That kicked off an intense couple of months for our family. Grace lived with our daughter at the hospital. Family and friends helped me out with our other kids. And an uncountable number of folks began praying for our daughter.

I'm headed toward a point about joy. But before we get there, I'd like to take an interlude on this prayer beat for a moment. This was a big deal. We had, I would guess, more than a thousand people praying every day for our little girl. Every now and again, I get the chance to speak in some other part of the country, and almost always a stranger will come up afterward to me to tell me he or she prayed and sometimes fasted for my daughter. We saw so many miraculous responses to these prayers—after the specialists ran out of ideas, they let us bring people to her bedside to pray, and each time she rallied within about ten minutes—that someone on the ward called the *New Yorker*'s science reporter to interview us.

But back to joy. During most waking hours, either Grace or I was at our girl's bedside. That could seem pointless to the naked eye, because most of the time she was in an induced coma. But we had a theory that people in comas can be attuned to the folks around them, at least in some deep, but very real, part of their spirit. So, right or wrong, we were pretty much always there, talking to and praying over our unconscious girl.

One afternoon I was there and her heart monitor started to beep. The nurse smoothly came over to our daughter with defibrillators and started to administer shocks to her heart. As he did this, he calmly said to me, "Mr. Schmelzer, her heart has stopped. We'll need to ask you to leave for a minute."

I called our church office to ask people to pray. I called Grace and updated her. And then there I was in the waiting area for about forty-five minutes by myself, not knowing if our daughter had died or perhaps had lived but with brain damage. No information. I tried to pray but the shock was too thick. After a bit, my fears began to make their way into words. If she was dead, what would that do to my relationship with God? What would that do to my relationship with Grace, as I knew that the death of a child is notoriously hard on marriages? I was the pastor of a modestly big church. Would I be a good model to everyone of how to go through something like this, or would I be a big letdown? And what could possibly be worth all this pain?

And then suddenly I felt as if God began to speak to me. It was something like this: *Dave, I'm not saying your daughter is going to die today. But let's say she does die. Would you rather that she'd never been born? You've gotten to know her for six months. Would you rather have skipped that so that you didn't have to go through the pain you're going through now?*

And I said back something like, *No, of course not. I'm hugely grateful for having gotten to know her, whatever happens.*

And God seemed to respond, *Great! And I'll tell you, she's hugely blessed by having spent six months on earth with you all. But if she dies today, I think you can take it to the bank that I'll be taking her straight into my arms in heaven, and you'll be seeing her again.*

And if she does die today, I'll tell you what you'll do. You'll grieve. And you'll keep grieving until at least that season of grieving is over. You'll love your wife and your kids. And you'll keep moving into life with me. That's what you'll do.

She didn't die that day. After many more harrowing days in the intensive care unit, some of which she spent hooked up to an imposing machine that pumped her heart and lungs for her, she was released to see if her improvement would continue. Now her intensive care was on our shoulders—her feeding tube, her daily vat of medications, her heart monitor. Over the next year she got better. Fully better. A heart that's normal. Height and weight right in the middle of her age range. A vibrant little girl.

What did I find at the center of that ordeal? Joy. Right in the middle of the worst experience of my life, I found a living, speaking, powerful, vulnerable God inviting me into a fresh level of connection with him and with reality in all its awe-inspiring and terrifying realness. Someone right there with me in the great times and the worst times, offering me resources where otherwise I had none.

Joy.

Some of my friends find this hard to take in. *Joy* in the sense of skipping down the street whistling? Maybe a better word is *connection.*

Or comfort.

Or intimacy.

But joy still seems like the right word to me.

At the time of my daughter's illness, being morally better than anyone else wasn't compelling. Even though I had a stake in teaching something helpful about God each week, suddenly being right about anything seemed like thin stuff.

Love was a pretty big deal, all the love I got from and— God willing—gave to Grace and our kids, and all the love we got from the hundreds of people who rallied around us. But right there in the abyss, at the very bottom, was God, joy in distilled form.

PART II

GOD

A Word from Our Lawyers

YOU COULD MAKE THE CASE THAT I'M overstating like a drunken man. So, on the advice of our legal department: Herewith, some disclaimers. One of the people whose answered prayers I've talked about in this book ended up leaving our church in a huff over a minor slight. Another one melted down pretty convincingly, and I see him once every year or so, only to have him vanish again.

And it's not as though *my* life is consistently such a powerful case for connection with this super-duper God. For someone who talks as much as I do about joy, Mr. Stage 4, why is it that a few times over the years I've mentioned to my wife that I feel as if my life has been squeezed out of me like water from a sponge, like I relate to Woody Allen's working title for *Annie Hall* (*Anhedonia*—the clinical inability to feel joy). (My wife's customary response to me at those times: "You're scaring me.") I've had my moments with online porn. On occasion, the money is a little tighter than I wish it were (yesterday, for instance). I get anxious on travel days as I imagine being on a plane with five little kids (also yesterday, for instance).

So . . . what exactly are we talking about then?

On Second Thought, Disregard Everything I've Said

I KNEW A MAN NAMED JOHN WHO, though no longer with us, was one interesting guy. He grew up in Appalachia, became a jazz musician, and hit his apex as an arranger and keyboardist for a big-time rock band in the early sixties.

His life hit bottom in the middle of all his traveling when he realized his marriage was near death. He and his wife, Carol, decided to file for divorce unless something changed soon. This wasn't a happy thought for either one of them because they really did love each other. But they were each a mess and it wasn't working and that was that.

That weekend John was playing in Las Vegas with the band, and in his misery, he decided to take a walk into the desert after the late show. In the darkness, John shouted out into the desert something a lot like what my Jewish friend had shouted in the shower: "God, if you're out there, I could use some help!" (Maybe that's the irreducible prayer. There could be a book in this for somebody—though it would be a short book.)

Just like with my Jewish friend, John felt as though he was all but knocked over, which convinced him he was on to something. With great excitement, he called Carol the next morning to tell her what had happened. But she interrupted him because she'd had an exciting experience of her own. In her discouragement over their life, she had gone over to talk to a friend the night before, and this friend had convinced her to pray to Jesus. She did it and had the kind of powerful experience that suggested to her that she'd gone to the right place.

Not long after this, John quit the band to start his new life with Carol and their kids. But he didn't have any real job skills. So after burning through the money they'd saved, he went from being a wealthy member of the rock-and-roll elite to a maintenance man who cleaned out oil tanks for a living.

One day an executive from his past life in the music world tracked John down at his work site. John hadn't been having the best day to that point anyway, and now this slick executive was peering over the top of his tank. The man stared down in disbelief at this oil-stained man who, not long before, had been a wealthy rock star.

"John," the man said. "What *happened* to you?" Not coming up with anything better, John responded, "*God* did this to me!"

Now God had done a lot of other things to him as well—putting his marriage back together, for example. And although John didn't know it that day at the bottom of the tank, within a few decades, he'd see as many miracles as just about anyone alive, meet some of the most dynamic people on the planet, and have more fun than he ever could have dreamed he'd have, even at the height of his fame.

But there was that moment in the oil tank, and that was real too.

Jesus invited people to follow him and, unless I'm missing something, that implies that we *go* someplace, and that we go someplace under Jesus' direction, as if we can count on his speaking to us. In the Gospel of John, Jesus promises that his voice will direct us places we couldn't have guessed on our own, places that will be unfathomably bigger than we could imagine.

You could make a good case that this thing—hearing the voice of God and responding to it—is at the heart of stage 4, which, you'll remember, I've called "mystical."

Now to educated and skeptical Westerners, this can seem odd, like a relic of a previous superstitious era rather than something that thoughtful people could believe in the twenty-first century. It might be worth noting that some of the great spiritual geniuses of previous eras have left us with incredible stories about direct communication with God. People like the amazing Teresas (of Avila, of Lisieux, and Mother, if with subtly different spellings of their names). Or Francis, of whom most thoughtful observers have quite a high opinion. Or the astounding Patrick of Ireland, who besides becoming a lovable character of folklore, is someone you seriously should learn as much about as you can, if you're the sort of person who has read this far in a book like this. Can I give you a brief bio of this great spiritual leader?

On the one hand, we don't know as much about Patrick as we might like, because he lived in the 400s. Happily for us, however, he irked church leaders in Rome enough that he had to defend himself in print, so we do know at least a bit about his life from his point of view. And the before-and-after picture of Ireland—and, within a generation, of all of Europe—is quite striking.

Patrick grew up in Rome-dominated England. His family was rich, but his fortunes spun around when he went out on a hike one day and got kidnapped by Irish slave traders. He was sold in Ireland and spent the next six years as a field slave. He had rejected the religion of his family many years previously, but his grandfather had been a clergyman and had helped Patrick memorize the book of Psalms. Now on those cold hillsides where he lived, Patrick found himself praying a lot of those psalms, to the point that he prayed a hundred of them a day—fifty in the morning, fifty at night. He got a nickname from the locals: "Holy Youth."

One night, Patrick felt as though he heard God's voice telling him something shocking: He should walk away from his slavery that very night and continue walking across all of Ireland to its eastern coast. When he got there, he'd find a ship that would take him back to England and his family.

Now there were notable risks he'd assume if he responded to this. In theory, he couldn't speak to anyone because his accent would give him away as a nonnative slave, and he'd immediately be returned to his master and killed for escaping.

Nonetheless, he went for it, and when he arrived on the coast, there was indeed a ship there. He had no money to pay for his journey, but the crew took him anyway, evidently because they were afraid that rejecting such a holy youth would put them on the outs with his God, and they might not survive their journey.

After some adventures (they initially went to France, not England, and nearly died from a number of different crises, some of which they survived because—we're told—God spoke to Patrick about what they should do), Patrick finally arrived home.

Not long thereafter, Patrick had another dream in which an Irish man said, "Holy Youth, return and walk among us." Ireland in that era was led spiritually by druids and was—in an understatement—lawless and wild. There was, for instance, human sacrifice. It's unclear if the Roman church had sent previous evangelists to Ireland, but if they did, all were killed.

To the dismay of his family, Patrick listened to the voice and returned. In doing so, he faced hard-to-imagine dangers and hard-to-imagine odds against making any difference. In his confessions, he says that he never woke up a single morning in which he didn't expect to be murdered that day.

Historians differ on the extent of the miracles Patrick performed, and it's not unusual for extensive legendary tales to grow up around the great spiritual leaders of that era. But it's clear to me that Patrick saw many impressive acts of spiritual power because he would have had showdowns with druids, whose whole shtick was based on miracles.

Patrick founded communities of faith all over the country, and by the time of his death, the *entire country* had swung to Jesus. Druidism was dead, and Ireland was now one of the most vibrant Jesus-worshiping nations on earth. In addition, Patrick also led a movement that abolished the slave trade there, the first known successful abolitionist movement in history. One man. How on earth did that happen?

Patrick wrote that his only spiritual secret was that he continued to pray a hundred psalms a day, just as he had on the hillside in his youth. His followers were so taken by this practice that after his death, they prayed 150 psalms a day, the entire book of Psalms.

After Patrick died, some of his disciples threw themselves into the sea in coracles—little round boats with no oars. If they didn't die at sea, they would preach about Jesus wherever they washed up. Europe, which at one point was largely Christian, had been overrun by neighbors and was now almost entirely pagan. Within one generation, these Irish missionaries reversed that. Writer and historian Thomas Cahill pitches that this sequence of events "saved civilization," as these missionaries also brought a number of social benefits with them: literacy, industry, and a love of learning.[4]

Until the mid-nineteenth century, people like the Teresas and Francis and Patrick were Western cultural heroes. They showed us how to know and experience God, and they pulled us through some of the worst patches of our history—including horrible religious eras like the Inquisition. They understood that the only way to make our way through religion gone bad was by the power and direction of the God that religion had left behind.

Our current discomfort with mysticism (or maybe, better said, our *recent* discomfort with mysticism, as there are a lot of signs that modern hyperrationalism is fading) kicked in in the mid-1800s as the Enlightenment had won the day in Western-educated circles, knocking people of faith back on their heels. The miracles of the Bible couldn't have happened because—*hello!*—miracles don't happen. If you can't dissect something, if you can't set up a reproducible experiment, it doesn't exist.

Church people responded to this disquieting turn of events in one of two defensive ways. Not wanting to look like fools, some conceded the point but began talking about Jesus' ethics rather than his miracles or his hotline to his Father. Surely we could agree that Jesus, at the very least, was a *responsible citizen*. Didn't that at least give us *some* leg up on the atheists? These folks became known as theological liberals.

On the other side, the religious antiliberals argued: Well,

hey, on these terms don't we have the *ultimate* scientific thing on our side, namely the *Bible*? You talk about truth that's good to the last drop! These folks got to work on splitting the atom of the Bible, trying to figure out what its fundamentals were as a rock to stand on against the onslaught of the atheists and the liberals. This perspective was also antimystical because God's actual voice to any given person couldn't hold up to the kind of scrutiny the atheists were bringing. By definition, such a thing would be *subjective*, which was the enemy. What the times called for was not that shifting sand of subjectivity but *objective* truth. This alleged objectivity (as—am I missing something?—can anyone besides God transcend his or her own actual experience of the world?) required some kind of pure reason, some kind of pure mind that looked at humankind from a plane beyond you and me. Logic—as formulated by Socrates and refined by Descartes and Kant—was the ticket, even to this new conservative religious movement of people who called themselves Fundamentalists.

For these folks, supernatural happenings and direct communication was out, but the Bible was in—hence a movement of churches that put *Bible* in their name.

Now of course there was the challenge that the Bible itself is filled with stories of miracles and prophecies and divine direction, all of which inconveniently happened to just about every single hero in it. The way out was offered by Englishman John Nelson Darby after he sat at the bedside of a wealthy female parishioner. The woman had a series of, of all things, prophecies while suffering from a high fever. These feverish prophecies suggested the novel idea that God had unrolled history through a series of what she called "dispensations." So, yes, all those Bible people did have direct experiences of God, but that was in a previous dispensation, a time when Jesus (and, earlier, his Father) had to prove himself to be God. Having proven it, there was no longer any need for such things. So—despite the long history of miracles and prophecies experienced by Jesus' followers—direct, subjective connection with God (evidently apart from the direct, subjective communication she was relaying at the time) or supernatural acts didn't happen anymore, and any claims to the contrary were, in the words of one of her most famous followers, "counterfeit miracles."

There was a countermovement to this as well, which started small in 1906 in Los Angeles under the direction of African American pastor William Seymour. Pentecostalism has now become the fastest-growing and second-largest of all Christian movements, but it has particularly taken hold in Latin America and sub-Saharan Africa, parts of the world looked upon with such scorn by some of our atheist Western writers.

Not all mystical faith in Jesus strikes me as stage 4. Far from it. But without direct communication with God—and direct action by him on our behalf—there is no stage 4. Which might be worth a longer look.

You—Yes, You!—Can Hear God's Voice

A FEW YEARS BACK—PRE-GRACE, pre-kids,
pre-pastoring—I was trying to make my way as a playwright in a competitive theater city. I was also giving about
twenty hours a week to lead a singles and young marrieds
ministry for about eighty people. I was leading a group
of about a dozen leaders. And I was working a part-time
make-a-living job.

Among my many challenges was deciding whom to
spend time with. Should I target a few of my leaders for
special attention? If so, which ones? One afternoon I prayed
about those things. I like to walk when I pray (combating
my modest narcoleptic tendencies when I'm sitting still),
and after a half hour or so I had some answers. As a throw-
in just before heading back to my car, I cavalierly asked
God if there were any women I should keep an eye on.

A few years earlier I'd had a serious girlfriend, but we had come to the end of the line when it was clear that neither of us could quite imagine marrying the other. Since then I'd had a few evenings out, but nothing beyond that. I had largely settled into long-term singleness, so this really was a quick last beat to my prayer. Yet faster than a blink, I sensed God saying, *Have you thought about Grace Coltrin?* And the honest answer was no.

I knew who Grace was—this belle-of-the-ball beautiful young woman who had just joined our church and my singles and young marrieds group. But I hadn't given her any thought because she was just a kid. It wasn't that I was so much older. I was twenty-eight and she was twenty-three. But that felt huge at the time. She just seemed very young.

So I replied, "No, but should I?" And it seemed to me that God said, *I'd keep her in mind.* So I did, although a few months went by before I invited her to lunch. We talked literature (something both of us had studied in college) and had a terrific time. I called her back a couple of weeks later and unwittingly kicked off about eight months of hell.

My interest in Grace pushed all sorts of her buttons. She liked spending time with me privately, but if she saw me in a public setting, she would openly shun me, looking the other way and walking past me if I went up to say hi. (She later explained to me that it was important to her to communicate to herself and her friends that I wasn't a boyfriend; I was just a friend like any other friend. Which, from my point of view, seemed to necessitate that she treat me far worse than she'd treat any comparable friend. To which she now responds: Well, touché.)

After one perfectly pleasant cup of coffee, she closed our evening together by saying, "Dave, if you think that we'll be friends for a while and then my feelings for you will suddenly change and we'll start to date, don't hold your breath."

It was hard to know how to take that in an encouraging way. After very little sleep that night (because, who was I kidding, I was utterly in love with Grace by this time), I went out for some tortured prayer that next day, which opened with my saying, "God, how do *you* interpret the words, 'Don't hold your breath'? I could be crazy, but that strikes me as pretty definitive. So I'm done with Grace." And immediately, he seemed to respond, *Dave, I feel the pain you're in. It's really horrible. But I don't want you to drop Grace. The woman doesn't know what she's talking about.* At that, I shouted at God. Shouted.

"Doesn't know what she's *talking* about? How much clearer could she *be*?"

Then God seemed to propose a deal to me. I should give him three months on this one. I shouldn't drop Grace, and no matter how much pain she caused me, I wasn't allowed to get mad at God. If I wasn't entirely happy with the way things were going in three months, I should feel free to yell at him until I passed out, to torrent him with bitterness. But not for three months.

About two months after God and I made our deal, Grace called me to talk. She said she was in love with me and felt so bad for how she had treated me. She hoped I would forgive her and she wanted to move forward if I would still have her. I would. We now have five kids together, and she remains heart-stoppingly beautiful and God's greatest earthly gift to me. And I hadn't noticed her once.

If I hadn't heard God's voice and if I hadn't met—or made things work with—Grace, I wouldn't have moved to Boston, continued my interest in fiction (I do a little novel writing), or taken the risks to start a church. Hearing God's voice has taken me into high-crime neighborhoods and into the halls of big money. I've seen horribly sick people get better. I've been pulled out of depression.

And that's just me. Grace has her own stories. My friend John the oil tank cleaner would have a five-volume set of stories. Today at lunch a CEO friend told me how an experience of hearing God during a recent worship time convinced him to walk away from his two thriving companies and head into new adventures.

Now let's not kid ourselves: Following God's voice can feel like a crazy way to run one's life, as John would have been the first to tell us from his oil tank. It feels deeply antimodern. And yet there's a certain part of each of us that invariably wonders if it's true, if there's a God we can connect with who is alive and active. A God who's not the removed God of deism but one who has the kind of perspective on our lives and futures that we could never have on our own. There's not a hero of the New

Testament (and much of the Old) that this God doesn't talk to at length. All the sages throughout the centuries who've made a difference to me would say that the only thing about them that might appear sage-like was their listening to and obeying the voice of an eminently wise and good God. It seems to be a part of the deal.

Maybe one way to think about this would be to wonder if God is *always* trying to speak to us, as if the only issue is whether we're tuning in, almost as if we're fiddling with a radio. This process of tuning in seems to vary from temperament to temperament.

I found my way in after reading a passage in the book of James, in which we're told that God will always give us any wisdom we ask him for, provided we don't doubt what we hear. That seemed to be both the encouragement I'd been looking for (as conversation with this God had been what got me into all this in the first place) and the ultimate disqualifier. On the one hand, it's a done deal! God promises to give wisdom upon request. On the other hand, we're not allowed to doubt that he's the one talking—and I've never met anyone who doesn't wonder if perhaps that quiet voice is his or her own. So we have a conundrum.

Here's how I tried to work my way through that conundrum. I decided to take nightly walks in order to test this out. I would start off with something innocuous, on the order of, "Hi God. How's it going?" (In my experience, he's always doing very well. For what it's worth.) Shortly thereafter, it usually felt as if God would return the favor and ask how *I* was doing. And then we'd be off, because there were always a thousand things I'd love God's wisdom about. So I would mention those things, do my best to wait for whatever perspective I could get, and then move on from there.

So, back to our original qualifier: How do I know that whatever I sense "from God" is, in fact, from God? The key answer: I don't. But here's what I've discovered—the more I hold that question in abeyance (as suggested by James), the more I seem to hear, and before long some surprising things are included, like the encouragement to keep an eye on this young woman named Grace.

Now who's to say I hadn't, at some deep level, already noticed Grace without it hitting my conscious mind? That in the stillness of prayer, I just unearthed my own desires? Could be. But that's not the way it seemed to me.

Listening to God's voice takes practice and patience for most people. Grace, for instance, didn't feel she was any good at this when we were first married. She was frustrated when she would hear me talk about things God had spoken to me. She was frustrated not because she didn't believe me but because she *did*. She wondered what was wrong with her that she couldn't find her way into this.

She finally found her answer when a friend told her that she—the friend—prayed much the way I did, except that she wrote out her prayers on paper. This friend was extroverted enough that she could never walk and pray as I do, because she knew she'd be distracted by everything she saw. But staring at a blank sheet of paper kept her focused.

She would write down questions very similar to those I prayed when I was walking. Then she would write down the first thing that came to mind that might be an answer. Like me, she had no idea whether those things were from God or not, but she made a deal with herself to not question it until she had tried this method for at least a month—her attempt at the approach James counsels us toward.

Grace pounced on this idea. Within about two weeks, she felt confident that she could pick out when God was speaking and when it might just be her own thoughts or desires. I've heard similar stories from many people.

Most folks I talk to agree that the Bible plays a key role in hearing God's voice, and they have developed an affection for reading it, learning from it, and praying through it, much as Patrick and his followers did. And those two things in tandem—two-way prayer and a love of the Bible (both of which, along with Jesus himself, incidentally get called "the Word of God" in the Bible)—can pack quite a punch. (And they do especially well when added into community, which gives us teamwork and perspective.)

I know someone who loved this kind of prayer and reading the Bible. She and her husband were doing doctoral work at King's College in London, and while they were there, they started a church for street people. But as they prayed, they became impressed with Jesus' saying that insofar as we love people on the bottom of society, we love him. They prayed about how to do that and decided to do a little digging in order to figure out what the world's poorest country was at the time. They learned that it was Mozambique, and after more prayer and counsel, they decided to move there. Then they went looking for the people who were at the very bottom even there, who turned out to be orphans. These children were often abandoned by parents who couldn't afford them, and they were found wandering the streets or living in dumps. So my friends started an orphanage and looked to start some churches around the country in the hope that communities of faith could help to address the many needs of Mozambique.

This couple burned out after several years there, took a brief sabbatical, got reenergized, and sensed God's direction to head back.

It turned out that God had a point. Today, perhaps nine years after that decision to go back, they've spearheaded a movement that has planted thousands of churches, fed tens of thousands of flood victims, seen many miracles (believe it or don't, they're some of the few folks I know who've prayed for dead people and seen them return to life), and continued to care for hundreds of orphans.[5]

How has God's continued, specific direction factored into all of this? They would laugh out loud at the question. They've banked *everything* on the voice of God. It's God's voice that has taken them to tremendous places of risk (I suppose moving to Mozambique in and of itself could qualify as a tremendous place of risk). But the risk was evidently contained by the God who had a role for them in the largest of adventures, the kind of adventure we all, at a very deep level, feel we're destined for.

Nobody Suspects My True Identity

I SAW AN ENGAGING MOVIE LAST WEEK called *Pan's Labyrinth*. It won't be to everyone's taste: It's subtitled (from Spanish), it's brutal, it's a little baffling (to my tiny brain, at least), and it's pagan (which I mean descriptively—*Pan* in the title is, well, Pan, as in the Greek god). But I liked it a lot. The movie begins with an archetypal story. A princess of an underground kingdom is curious to see the aboveground world. But when she arrives in it, she's blinded by the sun and forgets who she is. Now she just seems like an ordinary human, but someday, so the story goes, she will find her way back to her kingdom, be greeted by the loving king and queen, and take her place as the princess she truly is.

My wife says that's the fundamental fantasy of many a woman: that she's actually a princess but everyone is hiding this secret from her. A number of men and women have confided to me that at some deep level they believe they have a cosmic destiny. They may not share that with many people—who would?—but they know it's true.

I'm right on board with this. I feel as though *I* have a cosmic destiny.

C. S. Lewis actually opted to follow Jesus because of something related to this, something that propelled him into the rest of his life's work. He and his friend J. R. R. Tolkien had given their lives to studying myths. And Lewis knew enough about myths to know that they presented a problem to anyone considering faith in Jesus. Namely, one of the oldest and most prevalent world myths was that of the dying and rising harvest god. Given every nation's dependence on a good crop, was it any wonder that so many worshiped this god who, for the good of the community, died like a seed in the ground and then resurrected to bring fruitfulness no one could have dreamed of?

Tolkien answered Lewis so unexpectedly that it became the seminal moment of Lewis' life. To wit: Absolutely! That myth has indeed existed in almost every culture we know about, and yes, there's a striking similarity to the dying and rising Christ. But what if, rather than arguing *against* the reality of Jesus, it argues *for* it? What if that myth appears in so many cultures because God was preparing all of humanity for Jesus, helping us to know exactly whom we were dealing with? What if, as Lewis later put it, Jesus was "myth become fact"?

That line of thought not only gave us Lewis, one of the greatest English-language spokesmen for Jesus of the twentieth century (I suppose you could make a case in a different way for Billy Graham), it also led to a further fascinating line of thought that goes back to *Pan's Labyrinth*. (And *The Lord of the Rings*. And *The Chronicles of Narnia*. And many a Hollywood blockbuster.) Namely, the observation that there's one other universal myth, alongside that of the harvest god.

This is the hero myth. Plenty of people who have no love for God have spent a lifetime thinking about this perpetual myth (the most notable of these being Joseph Campbell), which continues to this day, mostly intact in almost all particulars, in infinite books and movies. Why have we been telling ourselves the same story over and over and over for—so far as we can tell—our entire history?

Well, just asking, but what if God himself implanted that story in each culture to tell us something profound about ourselves and about the human condition? What if God intends for each of us to take that hero's role in our own vast adventure? And what if, when we do, we'll find out why we've been created and about the actual stakes of the world around us? (This happens in every hero's journey—Frodo didn't know what was *really* going on in Middle-earth until he started on his quest.) What if this journey is intended to apply—with some customization—to men and women, teens and senior citizens, dads and moms? What if that's why we *like* movies (or sports)—because we're vicariously watching our own destinies play out without the risk of fully playing them out ourselves? What if, to put a nub on it, you're right—you *do* have a cosmic destiny?

This stuff runs deep. A few years back, I was watching the famously money-losing animated film *Sinbad: Legend of the Seven Seas* with one of my sons, who was then six. To my surprise, I thought the movie was terrific, realizing right away that it was a very intentionally rendered hero myth. The screenwriter was one of the writers of *Gladiator*, another archetypal hero myth. After the movie, my son—so struck by the experience that he was shaking—turned to me and said with chilling seriousness, "Dad, will you teach me to be a hero?" Quick as a blink, I held his gaze and said, "Yes I will."

I'm still working on how exactly to pull that off.

The hero myth involves a reluctant hero. He or she lives in what, to him or her, is the ordinary world, the world that's everything he or she knows. Little does he (I'll go with "he" because the character we'll track with is male) know that that world is actually in dire jeopardy and that he'll be called upon to take tremendous risks to battle the threat and return with the special gift that will heal and save this ordinary world of his. (If you're familiar with *The Lord of the Rings*, think of Frodo in the Shire, unaware of the tremendous storm of evil that's on the verge of sweeping over the whole planet.)

A call to adventure comes our hero's way. (Gandalf tells Frodo the significance of the ring and that Frodo himself must be the ring bearer.) Our hero says, "No way! Send someone else!" But often a mentor helps him get past those initial obstacles (Gandalf, in this case). Often, a "threshold guardian" pops up about this time (the Black Riders) to throw an obstacle in the way of our hero's attempt at crossing out of the ordinary world into a special world, where he doesn't know any of the rules and will have to improvise constantly (the vast world outside the cozy Shire).

But ultimately our hero does indeed cross the first threshold into that special world (crossing the Brandywine River into Bree). He faces tests and finds surprising allies and new enemies (the fellowship versus Saruman; the Elves—allies—and the Orcs—enemies). Midway along, he approaches an "inmost cave" that embodies some of his deepest-held fears, and indeed he faces an ordeal there that might all but kill him or even *actually* kill him (Shelob the spider's lair). Then there's some kind of resurrection and reward, ultimately followed by a sometimes harrowing journey back home to the formerly ordinary world to which he brings an "elixir"—the thing that will heal his land (the newfound courage and warrior spirit of the returning hobbits—now they can repel enemies from the Shire).

All this to say, what if you and I are invited into this special world, a world that will at first seem strange to us, where we'll need to improvise constantly? What if you and I are on a great quest that only we can fulfill and that has huge—if currently veiled—stakes for us and the people we love?

But what if saying yes to that call is a scary thing? The quest will include real suffering that we wouldn't face if we just stayed in the Shire, in the ordinary world (John suffering in that oil tank when he could have remained an unhappy but rich rock star, for example). But what if there's an unseen battle raging around us that, despite being unseen, is quite real? And what if the hero's journey—despite its difficulties and the nearly irresistible urge we feel to stay where it's familiar—is exactly what we've been created for? What if this journey will call out qualities in us we would never see any other way, and what if this journey, for all its hardships and challenges, is our only hope of ultimate satisfaction? What if *we* are that surprising princess or prince, invited into this harrowing but inevitable and satisfying road home?

If you were to run this by my friends in Mozambique, I think they'd nod and say, "You have no idea." Could the slave boy Patrick have guessed what was being offered to him when he first noted and obeyed God's voice?

Mother Teresa was a young Albanian nun on a train ride, reading the Bible to pass the time. Like my friends, she saw the passage about loving the worst outcasts from society as a means of loving Jesus. And then, like lightning, she felt God reminding her of her recent trip to Calcutta, where she had seen untouchables dying on the street. Saying yes to this call required Teresa to show great boldness and take huge risks. The type of order she proposed had never been commissioned by Rome. And who was she anyway?

Her only battle plan at the time was to gather people to go with her to hug these abandoned and dying untouchables, so at least they wouldn't die feeling unloved. But could she provide houses for these dying people? Could she provide doctors who could tend to them and either make their passage to the next life easier or perhaps even *heal* a few of them? Where would these houses and doctors come from? And she was a Catholic in a Hindu world. How on earth could she be anything but shunned?

By the end of her life, when hers was a worldwide order and she was a worldwide speaker, she must have wondered what fantasy novel she had drifted into. At her death, while the Western world was focused on mourning Princess Diana, Calcutta effectively shut down, as several million residents lined the route of the state funeral—of this Albanian Catholic.

This understanding—that we're invited into the role of hero in a much larger story than we could ever imagine—— has been central to what I've discovered in saying yes to this God.

If, say, the road of faith for Frodo entirely focused on succeeding in his ordinary world of the Shire, we would have quite a different story. Maybe Frodo, if he played his faith cards right, could be *mayor* of the Shire someday, the most respected person in town! But that's not the story we get; in fact, that role is vastly beneath what's being offered to him—and perhaps what's being required of him.

Finding this connection to an unexpected God while I was in college threw me for a continual series of loops. I had always assumed I would graduate into a stable, hopefully well-paying, but almost certainly uninteresting job. But once I met God, I suddenly had no idea where my life would head. So, doing my best to follow the thread that God was unspooling for me, I landed in a series of adventures.

As a first stop, I moved with a few friends to the community with the highest murder rate in the country. After a year there (and after getting to know several different families in which someone was murdered *that year*, not to mention being beaten up myself, along with experiencing the most vibrant neighborhood I'd yet lived in), I enrolled in a theological seminary. This seemed like a modestly more conventional step—right up until I started having a series of dreams, to my mind from God, suggesting that I should leave school a year early (with a degree but not the one I'd thought I was there for) in order to help out in churches and pursue a life as a starving playwright. I talked to seminary professors about this, and to a one, they said, "I've never said this before to someone I've really believed in, and I don't hear from God this way myself, but it sure sounds like God to me."

So suddenly I found myself working part-time jobs, volunteering in churches, and writing and producing plays. It was all interesting stuff, but it was also life on the edge, as I was, as advertised, *poor*. My plays both succeeded and failed, and it was increasingly unclear to me where my life was headed.

I was tired of always being asked, "What's someone like *you* doing here?" I was tired of always being faced with the terrifying prospect that, at my current rate, *nothing* in my life was going to change in a decade. Or two decades. Or more. I wanted a place in the ordinary world! And how had I gotten into this again? By listening for and acting on *God's voice*? If so, perhaps he could be so good as to get me out of this!

God was notably silent just then, but I came up with an idea nonetheless. I would go to grad school and get a PhD in literature so I could teach at a college. Did I *want* to do this? No. In fact, it barely interested me. But doing so would offer me something that I very much *did* want: this thing called a career.

I asked a friend who had already successfully gone down that road to help me pass the entrance tests. I studied for a few months, did great on the tests, got my recommendations in order, and prepared to mail them. But at that point, God decided to start speaking clearly. He said that it was fine with him if I went through with the plan, that I could still follow him, could still be part of a community of faith somewhere, and could still go to heaven. The only thing I *couldn't* do was live the life he wanted for me. But if I were willing to jettison that, by all means I should mail the applications.

I paced and fulminated, finally ripping up my applications, test results, and recommendations. It seemed that my only choice was to continue in utter uncertainty or abandon hope of the special, larger world. That day, continuing in uncertainty won.

Had I applied and been accepted, I would have resumed my schooling across the country the next August. What I didn't know at the time was that in September, while still living in San Francisco, I would meet Grace, the kind of fiery partner in this adventure of faith I'd given up hope of finding.

Not long after Grace and I got married, some friends asked us if we'd consider moving to Cambridge, Massachusetts, to start a different kind of church right in the shadow of Harvard. Arriving in Cambridge, we realized soon enough that if we really wanted to make a difference in this resolutely skeptical city, we could use some actual money. Although Grace and I were living well below the poverty line, I did have a modest inheritance from my grandmother. One of the founding eight members of our church was a young stock investor who had a penchant for taking bold risks. Grace and I had the crazy idea of asking our friend to take the small amount of money I had received from my grandmother and invest it. We gave him a year, explaining that we expected him to be bold and either make an immense amount of money with it or lose it entirely. We weren't looking for a 10 percent return. We wanted the kind of money that could give this new faith community a real launch or we wanted him to lose every dime. Would he be willing to give it a shot?

He was. He did, in fact, have a good feeling about one particular stock. If we were serious about our crazy scheme, he could put all our money into options, which would leverage our money tremendously and quickly leave us either loaded or broke. Is that what we wanted to do? Absolutely.

The stock our friend picked turned out to be the top stock in the United States the next year. We were in for a dizzying ride. One day I came back to our dingy, one-bedroom apartment and said to Grace, "Guess how much money we made on paper today?" The answer: a quarter of a million dollars.

With this infusion of cash, we started up a church and soon became a minisensation in Cambridge. We started with eight people, then grew to thirty, then perhaps a hundred and twenty, then two hundred, then five hundred, and on from there. The average church size in Cambridge at the time was in the dozens, so it didn't take long for us to get press coverage and the occasional press attack. I began getting invitations to speak in other parts of the country, sometimes to thousands of people.

Options trading did ultimately turn, as our friend had forewarned. On one memorable day, we *lost* a full million dollars on paper. For someone still living at a standard well below the poverty level, that was quite a moment. Yet astoundingly, it seems like a mere blip on the screen at this stage of things.

Our investor friend felt God's direction a few years back to do something radical of his own by leaving this church he had helped found and starting over completely in Manhattan. After tearful farewells, he, his wife, and about a dozen friends all moved to start a church in lower Manhattan, where my friend promptly lost all his family's money in stock dealings gone awry. Battery Park can be an expensive place to live for those with no money at all. They wondered if they should call it a day and return to Cambridge. They decided against it and prayed for God's provision not only to keep them all alive but also to do something supercolossal in an area not known for faith.

Shortly thereafter, a couple walked into their small church. The man was the personal money manager for one of the world's richest CEOs and was committed to empowering this little church to thrive. Not long after that, our friends met the head of marketing for a multinational company who pitched to them an ambitious citywide ad campaign aimed at people who'd given up on faith. Before long, they found themselves sitting at a catered dinner at the Ritz-Carlton with two hundred people who were open to reexploring faith.

I asked my friend how these things had happened to him—from destitution to overflowing wealth to impacting a city as seemingly impervious to impact as New York. He said he wondered if God just trusted him to say yes when these overwhelming opportunities came and that perhaps God knew he'd stay the course, whatever twists the road took.

What hopes do *you* have from this astounding God? My experience would suggest that he has much more in mind for you than you could even know to want—as Paul suggests when he prays that his friends would experience more from God than they could ask or even imagine. Hesed, again, suggested that God wanted to bring to us shockingly good surprises. But to be shocking, they can't be comfortable. Leaving our comfortable but small ordinary worlds can't happen unless we venture into a vast cosmic war that we've been blind to, maybe even intentionally blind to. And perhaps you've already made the connection between this special world and stage 4, in which we enter a world filled with truth that takes a lifetime to explore.

I think of Dietrich Bonhoeffer, who wrote *The Cost of Discipleship* just before his own life went into this vortex. His journey had him leaving his life as an aristocratic German scholar and pastor and becoming the leader of an underground seminary, training pastors who wouldn't swear allegiance to Hitler. He was ultimately martyred in a prison camp, but not before he won over some of his jailers and became a symbol of faith for the world. He couldn't have known what was in store for him when he wrote:

> The disciple is dragged out of his relative security into a life of absolute insecurity (that is, in truth, into the absolute security and safety of the fellowship of Jesus).[6]

With their passion for myth, Lewis and Tolkien discovered to their satisfaction that not only was the universal harvest god myth prophetic of Jesus but the universal hero myth spoke to God's deepest heart for you and me. There really was a hero's journey waiting for Frodo far beyond what he could know in the Shire. There really was a vast, epic Narnia just past the coats in the wardrobe, in which

Lucy, Peter, Susan, and Edmund were long-prophesied kings and queens. And this all wasn't far from what Ofelia discovered in *Pan's Labyrinth*.

But the hero's journey does bite back in one key way. It suggests that there's really no way to experience this powerful God if we resolutely stay in our ordinary world, our world that looks much like my pre-God dream of going to a good school, getting good grades, finding a good job, marrying a good woman, and dying with good money for my beneficiaries to enjoy.

God can certainly answer prayers in that world. We can join a church (or synagogue or mosque or ashram or spiritual society) in that world. But an experience with God of this scope? That's off the table.

Evidently My Options Are either to Be (a) Bored or (b) Terrified

SOME YEARS BACK, I WAS DRIVING ACROSS the country by myself. That wasn't a problem for me, to put it mildly. I had planned to visit a few folks on my journey, listen to audiotapes and new music, and have some time alone with my thoughts. It sounded terrific.

Two days into the trip, I was listening to the Bible on tape—the part where Jesus said that whatever we do to strangers in need, we do to him, and that those choices would even play into what happened to us, good or bad, after death. Just as I was pondering this, I passed maybe my twentieth hitchhiker of the day. Surely this couldn't be a suggestion that I pick up a hitchhiker? Whatever the safety risks of doing so might bring, I was more struck by the *solitude* risks—the sacrifice it would be to my personal space. After some pondering and some lurching prayer on the subject, I decided to dip my toe in the water by picking someone up for, at most, a twenty-minute ride. I promised God that after I left Iowa City the next morning, I would pick up the first person I saw and offer this arrangement—unless God broke in to warn me that this person was the rare but proverbial hitchhiking serial killer.

As I pulled onto the on-ramp to the interstate at about nine the next morning, there he was: a portly man with a down coat (it was August) and a suitcase, holding his thumb up. Ignoring the oddity of the jacket, I stopped for him. As he ran up to my car, he started shouting, "I DON'T BELIEVE THIS! I DON'T BELIEVE THIS!"

He explained that he had lost his job a few months back and hadn't been able to find a new one due to the bleak local economy. His brother was a churchgoer, but he himself had always been an atheist. Nonetheless, as he was pouring out his desperation, his brother had encouraged him to come to church with him and ask for prayer from the pastor. He had agreed and gone to church. That had been the previous day.

As they prayed, the pastor thought of something. From God? Who knew? But the thought was that my passenger should get the Sunday job listings from another city, someplace with a better economy, and start calling around. So right after church, my hitchhiker had found a copy of the Sunday *Los Angeles Times*. He had called in response to an ad for a paint store salesclerk. The person who answered had liked him but said he'd have to start by Thursday or there would be no job.

Of course the man had no money, so he couldn't figure out how he would get from Iowa to California in only four days. His brother encouraged him that this would be a good time for him to figure out if prayer worked. So he prayed that if there was a God, he'd get him to Los Angeles by Thursday. He and his brother walked over to the on-ramp to the freeway. His brother prayed for him and then left. I was the first car to come by. I stopped. I had California license plates. Hence the shouting.

"What part of California are you from?" he hazarded. I weakly answered, "Just east of Los Angeles," which threw him back into his shouts. I interrupted by saying, "Well, let's just see how it goes"—as my twenty-minutes-and-then-back-to-my-books-on-tape plan evaporated before my eyes.

"And what do *you* do?" he finally asked.

"Well," I responded, "I'm . . . studying to be a pastor." After some fresh exclamations, he said, "Look, I don't know anything about all this. I grew up as an atheist."

"As did I," I said.

"Well," he continued, "so what am I supposed to do?"

"About . . . ?"

"You know," he said, "about all of this. I guess it turns out there is a God. You're studying to be a pastor. This can't be an accident. What am I supposed to do?" I suggested he pray for a moment, saying in the prayer that he'd like to get to know this God who evidently actually existed and wanted to get his attention. And if he wanted to, perhaps he should also ask God to clarify Jesus' place in all of this. He prayed as directed.

We spent the next three days together, sleeping in the car and in the living room of some confused friends of mine in Las Vegas.

Bilbo Baggins, in *The Fellowship of the Ring*, says that the scariest thing on earth is stepping out of our front door, because we don't know what adventures we'll walk into. And ain't that the truth, particularly if we're listening and responding to this talkative God?

On a related note, one disappointing thing I've discovered in my unexpected life as a pastor is that some people get bored by me. Perhaps you can relate to them by this point in our narrative. They didn't think they would. It all started so promisingly. They dropped by our church and were taken off guard. I was so insightful and unexpected. But that was then.

Now, after perhaps five years of hearing my reflections on a lot of things about God, they feel we've played out the string. *Is that really all he's got? Could we do something a little . . . I don't know . . . meatier?*

I, however, am not bored by me. I'm confident I would be if I didn't spend so much time terrified.

I comfort myself that I've seen this dynamic in every church I've been a part of. After a few years there, some folks want something different, which usually boils down to one of two things: a deeper spiritual experience or fresh spiritual insights. I'm sympathetic; I want both of those things too. And yet my experience has been that these folks usually don't find whatever it is they're looking for. They visit another church, have an initial honeymoon there, and then move along again with the same complaint, like a restless spirit out of Dickens. It's an itch that's impossible to scratch.

Jesus is also sympathetic, but he offers a different prescription. He says that the sustaining food he eats, the "meat," as it were, consists of *doing* something rather than experiencing or learning something. And what he does is whatever his Father tells him to do in order to accomplish his Father's objectives on earth.

I've found those things to be what sustain me as well—of course conceding that how Jesus does this and how I do it are two very different things. My drive across the country took on a different cast once I felt God's prodding to change my plan and pick up a hitchhiker. But as I try to do such things, I always feel exposed and vulnerable.

I could think of plenty of stories along these lines, but one recent situation comes to mind. I had been pitching a six-week experiment in prayer and faith to some friends of mine, which they appreciated—so much so that they invited a number of their friends to try out this experiment as well—friends who weren't into God. I had never known folks who tried something like that and neither had they, which made them feel awkward. But they were persuaded—

as much as any of us ever can be— that God was prodding them in this direction, so they started inviting. After the initial awkwardness, all the folks they approached said they'd do it, and all of them did.

The group saw some immediate results. One woman wanted prayer for her son to get into a private school. However, the school was so expensive that it would cost more than half of what she earned. Clearly, even if he were accepted, he would need a scholarship—and the scholarship application deadline had already passed. Faith and prayer were entirely new to her.

You can guess where this is headed. After the group agreed to pray, the school accepted her son and offered him a free ride—again, this was after their scholarship deadline had passed. And also remember that this group of praying people largely didn't believe in God.

That encouraging development opened up a further conversation with this woman. As it turned out, a lot more was going on in her life than just this need for her son. She actually had an older son as well—but he had been tragically murdered at his job at a pharmacy. Someone had tried to rob it and attacked his supervisor with a knife. He intervened and was killed, saving the supervisor. This had thrown his mom into a year of near breakdown. She had tried everything to find some relief—Buddhist temples, hospitalization, grief groups—but nothing had helped. Perhaps my friends could help her?

They suggested she turn to this God who had seemingly

been so eager to answer their prayer on behalf of her other son. She did. I met her three weeks ago and she effused about how life changing her encounter with my friends had been.

Those friends are not in the group of folks who are bored with me.

This goes back to the hero's journey, wouldn't you think? Either there really is more going on around us than we think or there isn't. And either we really have a central role in that larger conflict or we don't. And if it's all true, either we say yes to that role or we turn it down and request new experiences or insights to alleviate our boredom.

Do you feel as though you have a destiny? Maybe a massive destiny? I agree with you! You've come to the right place! But you can't get from here to there unless you listen to and say yes to the direction of this greatest of leaders.

And that direction, in my experience, often involves taking risks on behalf of that scariest group of people on earth—strangers.

Jesus says that it's natural to love those who love us. The Mafia, for instance, has perfected that concept. The good stuff, the destiny-defining stuff, happens as we take chances in loving those outside of that circle. I know a number of people who are finding their way into some pretty large destinies, and they're all doing it on just those terms.

One friend and his wife felt God's continuing direction a few years back to move to a war-torn Middle Eastern country and then see how God directed them once they got there. They were the first Westerners to move there as the war was dying down. Not long after arriving, they met and befriended a few college students. One young woman brought her boyfriend by the house, and my friends got to talking a bit about their experiences with Jesus before ultimately praying with him.

Not long after that, they got a call from the young man's father, who turned out to be one of the wealthiest men in the country. *What had they done to his son?* My friend says his heart was in his throat—right up until he understood that the man wasn't angry; he was amazed. It turned out this man's son had lived a troubled life, burning through many thousands of his father's dollars every week in gambling. But that had all stopped; his varying troubles seemed to have cleared up. Again, what had my friend done to his son?

They got together to talk about it, and soon this man had his own life-changing encounter with God. He began to introduce my friend to his other friends, the type who ran the country. Today my friend finds himself making presentations about the teachings of Jesus during sessions of parliament in other Middle Eastern countries. He meets with kings. He's not bored with God, so far as I can tell. On occasions he's scared beyond scared. But bored? No.

And how did all this happen? He and his wife had no portfolio as they arrived in the Middle East. How did they begin to walk into what they would now regard as a destiny larger than they could have even fantasized about? They walked out their front door and listened as God directed them to make contact with strangers on God's behalf and see what would happen.

This is a time-honored, if rarely applied, prescription for walking into one's destiny, and it has a nice heritage, with people like Patrick, Mother Teresa, and my friends in Mozambique. And as the folks who were praying for the woman's son to get his scholarship to the private school discovered, this prescription has the surprising and helpful characteristic of working whether we formally believe in God or not. Whether we believe in God *afterward*, well, that's another story.

How Baywatch
Caused 9/11

I'VE HAD THE FUN OPPORTUNITY OVER THE past couple of years to speak to atheists' clubs at a local university. The most recent was a few weeks ago, and as you'd guess, the question-and-answer session at the end was lively. We looked at the claims of some of the recent atheist books and put them up against my alleged supernatural experiences. Why, for instance, do the most secular countries on earth—predominantly those in Western Europe—consistently rate high on social indicators: low crime rates, longevity, even happiness? If, as Jesus claims, it's "by their fruits you will know them," doesn't that convincingly argue *against* faith?

That was a tough one, but I wasn't in a mood to be pushed around by these cocky kids, so I pushed back. Yes, there clearly is a lot to be said for living in these countries.

Again, I'm not eager to live in a theocracy, so three cheers for what these secular governments do well!

But it isn't that *all* social indicators are so favorable there. Along with some recent blips on the race relations front, two indicators of note tend to fluctuate in those countries: prosperity and birth rate. A number of recent books have been released, pointing out the imminent demise of these cultures because their people have quit reproducing. Throughout Western Europe, the average woman has 1.5 kids. In Russia—which, of course, is not in Western Europe but is famous for atheism—60 percent of pregnancies end in abortion and the fertility rate is 1.1. (In the United States, it's 2.0.) It doesn't take a math whiz to figure out that if a man and a woman ultimately die and are replaced by their 1.5 kids, we'll soon be left with a whole nation that's older and, ultimately, gone. What's with these low-crime, high-longevity, relatively happy (if not as prosperous as they might like) people who are, nonetheless, in the long run suicidal?

One young man (the atheist groups I've spoken to have been made up almost entirely of men) had the beginnings of an answer for me. The true secularist, he explained, is not anthropocentric. Meaning that since people have no special place in the universe, we should feel free to either reproduce or not, and if a society dies out, so be it.

In my presentation, I had told some inspiring (to me) stories about heroic, faith-driven responses to Hurricane Katrina, so I hazarded, "To you, then, the tragedy of Hurricane Katrina is not so much that so many people were killed or driven away from their homes, families, and community. You're saying that that's no more tragic than, say, whatever damage was done to the coastline." He agreed with that and pressed his point by saying, "A person's death and a tree's death should have the same value in the big picture."

His response, I think, helpfully forces an important question that goes to the heart of Europe's slow population decline: How important are people, exactly? How can we answer that question? And what are the implications of our answer?

This is where not just God—as hesed-filled and astounding as this God is—but *Jesus* becomes interesting. Perhaps it's why the Bible makes the case that Jesus is irreducible in anyone's quest for a supernatural God, whether Christian, Muslim, Buddhist, or whatever.

I wonder if our road into thinking about this starts with Jesus' odd claim that he can forgive our sins. This was a major problem for me, and I've talked with countless others who also find this off-putting or medieval—or at the very least hard to understand. It goes back to the kind of moralism that sets up religion as something meant to make us into those good people we've never, to date, been. Again, I've met very few people who want to pursue that line of thought.

But to return to a question we asked a few chapters back, if the fundamental reality of the universe is *relational*, does this give us a different starting point? Most of us with any schooling at all have been taught that all "truths" are abstractions, but what if we were misinformed?

We get encouragement along these lines from unexpected sources. I'm no one's idea of a scientist, but unless I'm misinformed, I do know that quantum physics tells us that we can't understand the physical world without understanding the idea of a *vantage point*. As you observe something, you fundamentally change the reality of the thing you're examining. At a deep level, there's no way to avoid the effect of your very presence on the world around you. And so, in a strange sort of way, you're put into a relationship with the entire physical world.

If this is true, Jesus got there first when he said that he, not his message, embodies truth. Or when he suggested that sin and forgiveness are right at the heart of the universe.

When Grace and I got married, one thing we discovered was that, however well or poorly we might argue, it was extraordinarily hard for me to ever say I *meant* to do her harm. She might not like what I said; she might wish I had done something differently. But I consistently found myself saying in lieu of an apology, "However you felt about what just happened, I *meant* well." As you can imagine, that had its downsides.

During one particularly heated argument, I told Grace she was being outrageous and unhelpful, and she responded in kind. The argument escalated and I made a few more remarks that some might regard as cutting.

Later we discussed our fight with a friend who, to put a nub on it, went after me. She said, "Dave, are you sorry you said that cutting remark to Grace?"

"Well, yes, I regret it but, you know, in the flow of it, it made sense," I responded. "And the bottom line is that *Grace* said some outrageous things in the conversation too. In the heat of the moment, sure, I said something unhelpful. But look at the big picture!"

Our friend brazenly dismissed any interest in the big picture, saying, "No, I just want to know about that statement. You were effectively calling her a fool, and it's hard for me to understand how calling Grace a fool was meant positively."

She had cornered me, and I conceded her point.

"Okay then," she said, "if it's conceded, then are you *sorry* that you said something meant to make her feel bad about herself? Because what you said strikes me as *sin*."

She had me again. I said I was sorry and I asked Grace to forgive me, which she did. Isn't that the thing about sin and forgiveness? It's hard to actually move forward in life without this view of the world. Without it, our only options are scapegoating. Or the kind of stonewalling that I did. If we realize that there are problems in the world, and it's a given that *we're* not the cause of them, then the only thing we can do is *find* a cause to pin the rap on.

After September 11, 2001, you may have read one of the many articles speculating about why the conservative Islamic world was so mad at us. One that I read pointed out that the most popular TV show in the world at the time was—and this will make you proud of America's contribution to world culture—*Baywatch*. The article profiled one conservative Islamic town in Iran, a place where women wear burkas so as not to tempt—even by their hair—men toward sexual immorality. And now they have *Baywatch*, with Pamela Anderson in a swimsuit, and people are furious. They regard the United States as immoral both for producing such programming and also for having the cultural insensitivity to broadcast it into such a town. This, the article told us, is one of many factors that causes the Islamic world to hate us.

I told Grace that evidently September 11 was *Baywatch*'s fault. She replied, reasonably enough, "Well, I hate *Baywatch* too." But was there perhaps a little blame shifting going on in this line of thought? Whether or not the making of *Baywatch* was intrinsically immoral, was it being broadcast into this village against their will? Didn't some programming executive in their country make a decision to purchase this program? And when some local man was flipping through the stations and decided to linger on *Baywatch*, didn't *he* bear a part of the responsibility?

You could make a case that, if blame shifting is our only option, we are going to live in a lonely and explosive universe. And apart from sin and forgiveness, I haven't come up with another way to transcend this gloomy reality. As I researched my faith options in my early years, I discovered that the maestro of that quirky way into the universe seemed to be none other than Jesus Christ.

Yet again, I'm going to take a quick tour through the major world religions on this point. And let me again emphasize that no comment at all is intended on their worthiness or power. Instead, I'm looking to point out how truly strange Jesus' sense of personal mission seems to be.

So in my conversations and study, I learned that Buddhism, Confucianism, and Taoism didn't have much to say on this specific topic. While certainly in favor of people getting along, none of these nontheistic religions could offer a reconciler of the kind that Jesus presented himself to be.

Hinduism, as always, was more difficult to sort out. As such an ancient religion, it has developed a number of different pathways into the real. And one potential Hindu explanation for someone like Jesus, for instance, might be that he is an avatar—an incarnation of a higher being or maybe even the Supreme Being. (Some Hindus would talk about Vishnu this way.) But, however a given Hindu might account for Jesus, there still seems to be no figure comparable to him, no reconciler of his stature, no one who even claimed such a thing.

Historical Judaism certainly dealt with this. Sin and forgiveness were central, hence its famous system of animal sacrifices for sin. But that system was openly and unapologetically incomplete; it clearly hinted at something beyond itself. Do you know anyone sacrificing animals for their sins these days?

Which leaves me again with Islam, which offers perhaps the clearest and most intuitive symbol we have of the way sin is dealt with: by way of a scale of justice. You put your good deeds on one side and your bad deeds on the other, and at the end of your life whichever side wins, wins. If it's 51 percent good and 49 percent bad, good news! You cut it closer than is advisable, but you're in. This is a prime motivator of the duties of every Muslim—praying five times a day, taking a pilgrimage to Mecca, and so on.

At first blush, this strikes me as fair enough and—if this is the right word—manly. It also goes back to that fundamental impulse we've spent so much time talking about: establishing that we're good people. Yet while this is compelling legally, one wonders if it misses the mark relationally. What if life isn't just about what happens to us when we die but about experiencing rich—maybe ultimately rich—connection *now*?

At the risk of trivializing something so important, I remember, for instance, seeing an interview right after Frank Sinatra died. You'll recall that Sinatra, for all his great talent, had an occasionally unsavory reputation. Just after his death, I was watching a tribute show with some of Sinatra's cronies. It was rolling along well until one participant went off script with something like, "Well, Frank did have a temper. I mean, I remember one time he had a woman on his arm. I looked at her for a minute, and suddenly Frank was up next to me. His forearm was in my neck, I was against the wall, and four guys were coming at me. I mean, you know . . . that was a moment."

This unleashed an avalanche of similar, moderately horrifying stories. Finally the host, clearly uncomfortable, tried to find a way to divert the show back to its feel-good beginning. "All right, all right, all right," he said. "We all know Frank had a dark side. We all know that! But he was a great philanthropist. Whole hospital wings have been endowed with his money. The man was a great, generous friend."

Everyone robustly agreed with this, and the host closed by saying, "So in the end his good deeds obviously outweighed his bad deeds, and Frank is in heaven, can't we all agree?"

Indeed they could.

On scale-of-justice terms, perhaps we could go along with this, but I think we'd do so uneasily, feeling that this breaks down in ways we can't quite articulate. This can't be the whole story.

Let's go back to Grace and me. Let's say I make the same cutting comment to her as I in fact did, and she again calls me on it. And let's say my response is, "Grace, the fact of the matter is I do a lot of good things for you. In fact, yesterday I bought you four dozen roses just because I think you're a beautiful woman who deserves roses. And the day before, we saw a wonderful—and really *expensive*—theater production, which I'm sure you'll admit was really fun. I think it's obvious that my good deeds outweigh this minor bad deed, so drop it! We're moving on!" How might that go for me?

The scale of justice turns out to be the very thing that drove me from religion in the first place. I wasn't looking for self-righteousness—I had mastered that just fine on my own, thank you very much. I was looking for connection, hope, intimacy.

If Jesus is to be believed, connection is the most important thing, and alienation is the worst thing. His summing-up prayer for his followers is that they will be one, just as he is one with his Father. And he is remarkably helpful in empowering this kind of bone-deep connection. Suppose, for instance, that each moment of broken connection—each unresolved slight toward Grace, each angry thought toward a rude driver, each bitter reaction to life's rotten circumstances (and, implicitly, toward the God who doesn't bail me out of them all that quickly), maybe even each moment of vicious self-talk—builds up a little wall between me and the world, a little crustiness, a little barnacle.

Grace, for instance, might not divorce me because of any particular unresolved zinger. But if she's wise, she'd probably back away from me just a bit for her own emotional safety. Now imagine I've built up, oh, millions of those barnacles over the years, and that I'm now in a pretty dense cave of my own making. What hope do I have for a full, joyful life in this relational universe? How could I possibly dismantle that cave—presuming I had the insight to even *want* to? It's right at this point that Jesus raises his hand.

That's what so encouraged me and oil-tanker John and my showering Jewish friend. I have an acquaintance, a Muslim member of parliament in the Middle East, who was filled with despair at the prospects for peace in his country. What got him out of that? A connection with Jesus.

Nothing else had worked. And if Jesus is right, nothing else *can* work, because no one else is playing this game. It's not about being good. It's not even about being religious. (My acquaintance remains a Muslim.) It's about being connected.

By definition, secularism alienates, which to me, accounts for declining birth rates where it has most sway. And in a relational universe, people are ultimately important. The most relational picture we have of the spiritual world shows a God so committed to relationship with us that he made a very long and expensive trip to forward it.

And this might explain why the road into the kind of rich, supernatural life I've been pitching *has* to start with our chatting with God and responding to what we sense he says. This might also explain why the religious response to modernity has felt so unsatisfying for so many. It puts faith into the category of "being right" about something, about proving or disproving something. And as we've said, being right has fewer rewards than we might have supposed.

I Want Lots and Lots of Sex

I HAD A MEMORABLE CONVERSATION WITH a fellow pastor a while back. He pulled me aside at a gathering and said, "Dave, I love how you're always so positive when you talk about God. But . . . I mean . . . when do you get to, you know, the bad news?"

I wasn't sure I was tracking with him.

"You know," he continued, "the bad news. The fine print. The stuff, you know, that you have to *give up*, for instance."

"Stuff like . . . I don't know . . . addictions? Trolling for porn on the Internet?"

"Yeah. Sure. Stuff like that."

I thought for a moment and said, "Well . . . I guess I haven't met many people who've said to themselves, *You know what I want to be when I grow up? A porn addict. Because they have such great lives!*"

It seems to me that it's easy to fall into a view of God that's something like this: Picture a beautiful Alpine valley on the best of days. And there's God in the middle of this spectacular valley inviting you to join him. And you do! It's just unbelievable. You wonder why you didn't do this sooner. He continues beckoning you further on into this awesome scene, but this time he asks you to follow him around a corner. You follow him . . . and then he hits you over the head and steals your wallet.

One of my great surprises in this spiritual journey is that there seems to be no downside with God. I thought that there would be. I vividly remember—just after admitting that God appeared to be real—thinking that, of course, I should hedge my bets. Obviously. I was just hitting that phase of life when it was quite possible to sow my oats. I was starting down an educational path that could potentially lead me to some real money. Both of my roommates were evangelists for the benefits of recreational drug use. While I was increasingly sold that Jesus could deliver the goods, I was also sold that going down that path too heedlessly might cost me a lot of what anyone in his right mind would regard as the good stuff in life. So I was stuck.

I did pray a bit about it, prayer having been so helpful for me up to that point. I continued reading the Bible here and there, and increasingly it struck me that this really was an all-or-nothing choice. And that the only way choosing Jesus made any sense was if there was zero bad news in what he said.

Sex, of course, was the first hurdle. Rumor had it that sex outside of marriage was discouraged in the Bible. How should I think about this?

Well, first, I supposed, I should check out that claim for myself. And I found that indeed, here was one instance where the popular conception wasn't a misconception. Now Jesus did unsettle us just a skosh with stories like the one about the woman who was caught having sex with a married man and was nearly murdered in a hail of stones. Famously, he seemed to take her side rather than the side of the murdering moralists, and it's things like that that make him so likable. But he didn't call them prudes and he didn't overturn their standard. His closing words to her were to "go and sin no more."

Now even that has some real texture to it. Was his point that, if she *did* in fact sin in this way another time, he would have to join the gang with the rocks? That doesn't sound right. His point wasn't that she was a sinner in her way and her accusers were sinners in their ways, and now the homework assignment was for them to go off and get their acts together and find him when they did. What if he wasn't admonishing her but encouraging her? What if he was saying, "Hey, look, you'll discover that you now have the *power* to quit doing this destructive stuff! Take advantage of that!" As if this behavior was never in her best interest in the first place, however strong its allure.

I think we can buy that, if we give it a moment's thought. Forget moral judgments. How many women, even today, would say that it's a good idea to sleep with a man who's married to someone else? Who would say that sounds like a terrific path to the happy life they've been shooting for?

It's said that men reach their sexual peaks at nineteen. I got married when I was twenty-nine. That created a pre-scription for some real soul-searching on this topic. Was this, in fact, the fine print, the bad news, that my friend was talking about?

I'm sorry to say I have no brilliant answers on this sub-ject, despite the fact that as a pastor, people do tend to bring it up with me all the time. But I do believe one thing: The only way anything I've been talking about works for the long run is if we become utterly sold on the idea that God only brings good news. As soon as we allow that sometimes he doesn't, we're sunk. For one, that belief would cut to rib-bons the central claim of the Bible.

And encouragingly, I've found this to be actually true, and my friends have found this to be true, and many of the people you respect most in history have found this to be true.

As I struggled with this issue of sex in my twenties, I decided to cast my fate with God. This is a struggle that uniquely targets young men of that age, so it may not be your struggle. But perhaps some things will have transferable value to you by analogy.

So, despite having some really wonderful serious girlfriends along the way, I made it to my wedding night having stayed on this track. Grace has said that's a huge deal to her.

But that's not to say there weren't any number of tortured moments along the way and that there's not the occasional tortured moment now. As I mentioned, my preministerial life had me working as a playwright for many years. In the middle of this, like many people serious about life in the theater, I visited New York to scope out a possible move there. This was in the pre–Rudy Giuliani years before they cleaned up Times Square, where you go if you want to see Broadway plays, as I, of course, did. So multiple times a day, I would walk past a number of strip clubs with large, explicit, backlit photos and hawkers who would run up to me—a man walking by myself—and all but *drag* me inside, with promises of the paradise that was through those doors. After fending off, I don't know, an infinity of them, my will to resist was gone. I was in my midtwenties. I was staying away from sex. At that point, I didn't have a serious girlfriend, so a sanctioned end to my sex fast was not imminent. And I had anonymity! I was in a city three thousand miles from my own so I knew I wasn't going to run into my uncle Edgar in there. No one would ever know! What could *possibly* keep me from letting the guy drag me in?

That thing that could keep me out of the club turned out to be simultaneously surprising and predictable—God's voice. I kid you not. The hawker was pulling at me. I had already decided that this time I was going in, whatever qualms I might have had previously. But as I took the step toward the door, I got a strong sense along the lines of, *Dave, have I let you down once? Ever? Don't I have a history of coming through with my promises to you? What makes you think that this promise, however difficult, is the one part of the Bible where I'm out to get you?*

I pulled myself away from the guy, headed to the first subway stop, went uptown thirty blocks to the park, got out, and thought I'd rather shoot myself in the head than keep going like this. And yet, as I nonetheless talked to this communicative God, pouring out all my bitterness on this subject, I felt better. No, "better" doesn't quite capture it. I actually felt encouraged that this was going to end well, despite these bumps in the road. I felt much as I would those years later when I spoke with God about Grace telling me not to hold my breath—namely, that I should give God a few months without yelling at him about this latest frustration and then see if I wanted my money back. I did that that day in Central Park. I don't want my money back.

That God is a genius, if you ask me. He's capable of spouting out only good news. And it's terrifically helpful that he's so willing to be right there for us as we hit these rough patches.

And who knew? There's more! When referring to marriage, the Bible does an abrupt about-face and encourages all the hot sex you can manage, and that's been a very nice bonus. (Check out Song of Songs for the steamiest sacred literature I'm aware of.)

Now, of course, what if God *hadn't* had someone for me? Could I have sustained the sense that it was all going to turn out well for *decades*? Could this God make even *that* scenario okay?

I was so taken with what I learned about Saint Patrick that I spent a few years by and large taking his prayer pre-scription. "By and large" in that I prayed a mere twenty-five psalms a day. But even that was a transforming experience for me, as it guided me into a prayer journey that I didn't direct, one that promised to help me understand and experience the things that were most important to God himself.

And it was hard to miss that perhaps a quarter of the psalms begin with a command *to ourselves* to praise God, whatever is happening in our lives, good or bad. Should I praise God, say, for my sexual frustration as I'm tearing myself away from the strip club hawker? Should I praise God for all my big dreams that show no signs of coming to pass? For those years slipping away when I'm not married? Or, God forbid, should I praise God for genuinely tragic things? This is worth a longer look.

PART III

HAPPINESS

I Was Pretty Bummed Out Yesterday

HERE'S A PROVOCATIVE ITEM from Slate.com I read this week, as paraphrased in my local paper.

Data show money doesn't bring happiness. That's led some economists to move beyond money, to study happiness itself. A recent large-scale study revealed that we start out okay, but from ages 16 to 45 there is a steady decline in happiness. How unhappy? Unhappier than if our incomes were suddenly cut in half. But it gets better. After the age of 45 there is a remarkable 15-year upswing in happiness, making us happier than if someone had suddenly doubled our income. So, how do we climb out of the well of unhappiness? Economists can only speculate, but believe it's got to come from all that wisdom gained in the trenches.[7]

As I write this at forty-four, it's great to know I've got good news just around the corner!

One would think that, if this God is as good and as powerful and as available as I've been pitching, it would make some impact on our happiness. And yet just exactly how that's so is often less than straightforward. A number of folks have taken a swing at this question, most notably C. S. Lewis, who wondered if we should factor in one's starting point. So, yes, many a secularist might be happier than many a person of faith, but perhaps they started at very different points—genetically, in life circumstances, and so on. What Lewis found to be true, however, was that, at the very least, people who have found their way into a life of living faith should be happier than they were beforehand. It should make a difference.

But others would pitch that the question itself is a false lead. I've just finished up the magisterial *Happiness: A History*, by Darrin M. McMahon, and he points out that before the Greeks, the idea of a happy life was one with minimal catastrophes, leading to the aphorism, "One can count no man happy until he is dead" (as one never knows what turn of fortune awaits).

McMahon says the Bible takes a dim view of our hopes for earthly happiness. By the time we get to its last book, John's Revelation, we see a horrific world of battle and destruction in which the victorious get to enjoy a great *afterlife*. We get encouragements like "The one who endures" will get any of a variety of great things that don't offer us much in the here and now. One thinks of, say, Jonathan Edwards, who wrote a series of life resolutions when he was nineteen, one of which was:

> Resolved: To endeavor to obtain for myself as much happiness *in the other world* as I possibly can, with all the power, might, vigor, and vehemence, yea violence, I am capable of, or can bring myself to exert.[8]

It was, McMahon pitches, during the Enlightenment that people began to persuasively ask why we can't hope for happiness *now*, afterlife be hanged. So we get famous milestones in this line of thought like the familiar refrain that governments owe their subjects the opportunity to pursue life, liberty, and the pursuit of happiness—a shot over the bow of how any government had seen itself before. McMahon points out that within the first hundred years of this new republic, Americans had filed more lawsuits per capita than had ever been seen, presumably because their promise of happiness had been foiled.

And so here are wretches like me—sold out to the idea that God has great stuff in store for me and firmly situated in the Enlightenment mind-set that, all things being equal, I'd like to be as happy as possible in *this* life, thank you very much.

As I've pointed out, I don't always find that to be the easiest thing to pull off, despite being connected to this active, powerful, good God who is so eager to offer such startling experiences of joy. So most people I know find that an astoundingly answered prayer is good for about a two-day happiness boost. When my daughter was sick, I remember thinking that her getting well would blow the doors off anything else I typically worried about. If she got well, who really cared how my church grew or my endless petty ambitions fared?

And for a good month or two after her miraculous recovery, that was just how I felt, which strikes me as pretty impressive.

So what impact does this God have in the way our lives *feel*, which can seem quite close to how our lives *are*? Or should we just hang in until we're forty-five and let nature take its course?

We get a provocative hint from Paul, who cryptically tells us that he has learned the secret of contentment, whether he has a lot or very little. As if *The Da Vinci Code* is right and there's some secret knowledge that only the super-spiritual are privy to. At the very least, it gives us a target.

I ask people all the time to tell me their secret of happiness. I get answers like generosity, which strikes me as a good one. It does seem as if Scrooge, by definition, could never be happy. The root of *miserable* is "miser" and so on. And hesed pitches that right at the heart of *God* is unaccountable generosity. As if our own stream of generosity taps into something right at the center of the universe.

I know some phenomenally generous people and I've heard so many stories of generosity followed by unexpected windfalls that to me it's a lock that those things are connected. And yet even so many of these generosity paragons struggle with day-to-day happiness, so we must need a little more texture than this.

My favorite professor taught powerfully about Paul's mandate to "fight the good fight of the faith." As if every day we're assailed by spiritual darkness and our task is to fight for belief in God's promises over our lives until our hearts are happy in him. I'm all over this, and I feel as though this is often my daily task. And yet there is a slogging-through quality that this can bring, as if each day is a battle. And if Darrin M. McMahon is right, that may well be the point of view the Bible is pitching.

In my quest for happiness, many have recommended that I take seriously the quaint biblical idea of observing a Sabbath day. I remember the first person I met who did this. I was in school and finding the schedule to be demanding. And here was this young woman who wouldn't study on Sundays because it was the Sabbath day. How on earth could she survive academically? Quite well, as it turned out: She graduated with honors. And she claimed she had received the gift of joy along the way, the joy of believing that God himself would back her as she received the restful life he wanted to give her. She sold me. I do this.

Some of my friends extol the blessings of spending time with other people of faith, pointing me to the advice later on in the New Testament to "not neglect our meeting together." Among other benefits, when you're down, you can ask your godly friends to pray for you, which is a powerful way to cheer up.

This practice has a special place in my heart, as someone who entered ten years of on-and-off mild depression *after* I started pursuing faith. Strangely, I actually think those two things were related. Before I experienced faith, feeling *anything* was too threatening for me. But suddenly I had the safety to feel again, which meant that I often felt *bad*. I prayed through this, briefly talked with a counselor, and got encouragement from my unfortunate wife.

But the turnaround came at an unexpected time. Grace and I were part of a small team looking to plant a church. We had all just met one another, and as we entered into one of those early meetings, I felt my familiar gloom. Grace—having a sharp eye for this—checked in with me on a break. I told her that the reverberating thought in my head was that no one there cared about me at all. With her customary wisdom, she sharply told me that was absurd and that I needed to share that pernicious thought with the group. Dutifully, I did this and the group immediately prayed for me. One of the quieter members prayed something I can't recall, but as she did, I felt something happen, a lightness that was unfamiliar. I excused myself, went out to pray a bit and get God's perspective, and have never felt that depression again. I'm a believer in pursuing this life with others.

And there's so much more that's worth keeping in mind, which can make it all feel too complicated and helps us understand why Paul might have trumpeted that he had found a *secret* to contentment.

As I mentioned, the psalms counsel us to praise God in everything, good or bad. You can imagine how that got put to the test, say, in our daughter's sickness. But we went for it nonetheless and discovered real power as we did. It's comforting to know that God is with us and is good just as our lives are *today*, that we don't need to wait for some imagined preferable future in order to experience God's loving us moment to moment. It seems that praising God is *always* the way most people get to this comfort.

Perhaps the most powerful of all these strategies is also the most humble. One friend says he likes to ask God each morning for a great day, the kind that he'll be happy to have lived as he lays his head down on his pillow that night. And he claims that God is only too glad to answer that prayer. I think my friend is right.

But maybe the deepest wisdom comes from theologians who argue that we live in a time that might be called "the now and the not yet." As we connect with this most powerful and most good God, Jesus tells us that "the Kingdom of Heaven is near." These deep thinkers wonder if, at the moment of that encounter with God, it's as if heaven itself is right over our heads, separated only by a thin membrane. And to push the metaphor, what if heaven has a lot of heavenly water in it, and in our nearness, we sometimes get splashed with big drips sneaking through that membrane? If this is true, then because of our connection with this astounding God, we can get tastes of heaven right now. In heaven, presumably no one will be sick or miserable. So, sometimes—*drip!*—we get spontaneously healed right now. Or sometimes, after many false starts, a gracious person prays for us and we realize we're no longer depressed.

And yet there's also the "not yet" part. Because the Kingdom of Heaven is only *near*, we don't get to live there just yet. So McMahon is right in his understanding that a good deal of life today is a kind of struggle side by side with this powerful God, as if there will be that constant need to praise God no matter what and to invite our friends to pray for us and to ask God for great days and to turn our problems over to God. And to some degree, to whistle past the graveyard, to recognize that happiness—except perhaps for the occasional sunny temperament—has never been easy for anyone. And maybe that's not the worst thing, because it invites us into continued, deep connection with this good God, and into continued, deep connection with others who love him.

And there is in fact an offer of sudden joy, of sudden delight, that's held out to us in the best times and in the worst times, and how bad can that be?

This calls me back to the thought we opened with, that maybe our task isn't so much to be "right," to find The Answer, as it is to be "on to something" real that rewards exploration.

On the other hand, I'll be forty-five soon, so get back to me in a few years.

Sometimes My Prayers Feel Pretty Lame

WHEN THE REPORTER WAS INTERVIEWING Grace and me about the remarkable answers to prayer that we had seen for our daughter, he pressed in on one troubling part of the story.

One of the outcomes we had been eager to avoid was the use of a machine that would pump her heart and lungs. While it could save her life, it could also push her one step closer to the end. On several occasions, the doctors felt she was failing to the degree that she needed to go onto the machine, but each time we asked for an extra hour so we could ask our hundreds of praying friends to pray against this. The doctors always agreed, and each time she improved so notably that ultimately someone called the *New Yorker*.

Right up until she didn't and she had to go on the machine.

The reporter asked if this had embittered us against prayer. If the thing we had wanted to avoid ultimately happened, didn't that shake our confidence in these prayers? My response was that the last thing I wanted as she went on this frightening machine was for people to *stop* praying for her.

But—asking you to grant, for the moment, my belief that prayers are frequently, astoundingly answered—why aren't they *always* answered? Why do bad things happen to godly people?

I've thought deeply about this, and I think I've come up with a satisfying answer: Beats me.

I mean, you'd think it might have something to do with "the now and the not yet," wouldn't you? And traditionally at this point, someone inevitably mentions something about the first part of the Bible, which talks about the many bad consequences of humankind's rebellion against God, and I'll defer to my elders on that one.

But whatever the explanation, it seems unarguably true that we do in fact go through hard times and that prayers— while always, always advisable—don't always remove us from suffering as quickly as we'd wish.

Here's an image that, while perhaps a bit fanciful, strikes me. We get this picture at the end of the Bible of a bowl filled with incense, which we're told is the substance of our prayers. At some point the bowl fills up, at which time an angel takes it, tosses its contents into a fire, and big things happen on earth—earthquakes and the like.

So just for grins, let's take this picture a step further. What if each thing we pray for has its own bowl in heaven, as it were? And what if each prayer we pray on that subject finds its way into that bowl? When the bowl is full—*shazam!*—our prayer is answered. And what if the bowls all have different sizes? So let's say I have a head cold and you pray for me and, goodness gracious, I actually do feel better afterward. On this theory, that's one size bowl, and your prayers filled it. Let's say, conversely, that we pray for peace in the Middle East. Can we agree that that's a bowl of a different size? But the key thing here is that peace in the Middle East does *have* a bowl—however vast, it's still finite. So hypothetically, if we got millions and millions of people to pray about that every day, perhaps even that bowl is fillable.

I've had some memorable experiences on this front, both great and humble. A few years back, I was praying for our church when God broke in to encourage me to pray for a friend who was going through some hard times. This friend had some long-standing bitterness toward God, and I had prayed plenty for him in the past with no visible results. But this time God seemed to be suggesting I had vastly underestimated the size of the prayer bowl we needed to fill in order to see results with my friend. It was as if the wounds from both his life and his early church experiences were far bigger than I could guess. From that prodding, I ended up praying about a half hour a day for my friend over the next six weeks. I also fasted quite a bit for him (many great saints have felt that fasting fills these prayer bowls as well).

About three weeks into this, I got a call from my friend. He wanted to tell me about the good things happening at his church—so far as I knew, he hadn't been in a church in decades. While there have been some bumps along the way, this connection to God has continued for my friend.

Prayer bowls.

And I've had memorable intersections with this thought on grand scales as well. Take this for what it's worth, but I had an odd experience just before apartheid fell in South Africa. My friends took me to see a movie called *A Dry White Season*, a movie whose goal was to implicate the audience in the horrors of apartheid. Its point was that benevolent, nonracist, liberal onlookers were just as guilty as the Afrikaans police officers who destroyed black townships. Once you were aware of just how bad apartheid was—and the movie had just made you aware—if you did nothing, you should prepare for a comfy eternity in hell.

I was ticked off. My friends cheerily debriefed the movie, talking about the merits of Marlon Brando's South African accent and whether the movie dragged in patches.

And I found myself shouting, "Are you out of your *minds*? Were you watching the same movie as I was? They don't *care* if you *like* it! It's a trick! They lured us into the theater, took our eight bucks, and now they've implicated us in *apartheid*!"

My friends looked at me blankly for a moment until someone hazarded, "I thought Susan Sarandon was great."

At a worship service the next day, I couldn't get apartheid out of my mind. Was I supposed to post myself on my congressman's door? Was I supposed to quit my job, travel to Johannesburg, and get a job in a mine for solidarity? And then the thought hit me—perhaps from God?—that one thing I could do, as someone who had seen some great things happen through prayer, was pray for South Africa every day until apartheid fell.

Three months later apartheid fell.

Bloodlessly.

Miraculously.

While I'm of course tempted to say, "Now you know who to thank," I'll refrain. Clearly a lot more was going on there than just my prayers. But what if it's true that a lot *less* than my prayers was going on there? What if there's a God who calls people all over the world to join in prayer for things that are clearly on his heart? What if that's a part of how the world works?

I wonder if such thoughts go back to our early question about whether or not God has a permanently furrowed brow about all the awfulness always happening in the world. I recently read a collection of essays from secular authors on the book of Job. In each case, the author's bottom line is that Job proves what any rational person could clearly see to be true: God is either a fantasy or a sadist.

And yet there are those billions of people who, like me, have wandered into a world with a God who is clearly anything but either of those things. So perhaps another perspective would suggest that the awfulness in the world—and, on occasion, in our lives—proves something different. As the hero's journey suggests, what if we're actually in the middle of a battle far bigger than we could have guessed? Job itself suggests as much, if in a poetic fashion that can make this battle seem capricious.

Now *why* we find ourselves in such a battle is beyond the scope of what I want to chat about here. But let's say the battle is real. And that we're offered tremendous resources in this battle from the home office, along with an extraordinarily present and courageous commanding officer. And that one of our two primary weapons (along with active, aggressive, sacrificial love) is this potent connection offered by prayer. Sometimes those prayer bowls are quite big, and the battle around the issue at hand is quite intense. But from this perspective, we realize that all the wars and injustices demonstrate that we are in fact playing for real stakes. On this theory, we shouldn't be surprised at these things. Rather, we should engage with them in every way possible, prayer included, rather than standing at a distance and judging God.

A local professor who's an outspoken atheist recently argued that prayer is immoral. That struck me as unaccountable. Immoral? *Misguided* I could see, as of course this professor denies that there is any recipient of these prayers. But what on earth could be the harm in praying?

Well, he answers, all that time spent praying about tragic or unjust things could better be spent *addressing* those things. Prayer is a sop for folks who don't actually want to engage with the evils of our world.

This is quite a boggler to me, since it seems like the great majority of the people in world history who have most loved the suffering have been praying people. I'm in touch with several hundred praying people who continue to do tireless work in post–Hurricane Katrina New Orleans, for instance. For many people, prayer and love are profoundly connected.

To punt back to my "now and not yet" theme, whatever our situations in life, we are offered real connection, and possibly real joy, right where we are. In the end, of course I can't answer why we live in a world of such suffering any more than I can answer why we're offered this powerful connection to such a good and present God. But I do know that both things are true and real. If our emotional response to the pain of the world is to disengage from, curse, or mock the thought of a caring God, fair enough. But in my mind that's our loss. If our prayers are still spectacularly unanswered—as some of my most pressing prayers at the moment do seem to be—we're nonetheless given the opportunity to experience this good God right now, *along* our journey rather than at the *end* of it. If our daughter was going to go on a heart-lung machine despite our prayers for a different outcome, well, that was reality. I'd just as soon go through that reality with God than apart from him. And I'd rather that she receive as much prayer as possible along the way, because her grave illness did, in fact, *have* a prayer bowl, however big it might prove to be.

Your prayers matter beyond what you could guess, whether you're seeing those prayers answered now or not. In my mind, this world of suffering isn't going anywhere. But—as hesed suggests—as we faithfully pray (and love), we will see many wonderful surprises.

Isn't Faith Always Just One Step from Being Disproved?

FAITH, FOR ALL ITS ALLEGED POWER, CAN seem like a dicey thing to bank one's happiness upon if one, say, reads a newspaper. For instance, a few months back, the Discovery Channel made two big announcements. First, they said that *The Lost Tomb of Jesus* was their best-rated show of the year. This was the exposé in which *Titanic* director James Cameron announced that almost certainly he and his friends had found the tomb of Jesus, his son, and his wife (Mary Magdalene) and that, therefore, faith based upon the New Testament was now refuted. Then the Discovery Channel said they wouldn't re-air it and had no further comments about it. This seemed to be a new record for how quickly a network could heavily promote the latest shocking finding about Jesus and then cut it loose.

These exposés about faith seem to be coming at an increasingly rapid clip. We had, of course, the granddaddy of them all with *The Da Vinci Code*, whose shocking claims about Jesus ended up being cut loose by the loudest secular voices in the country.

Then we had *The Gospel of Judas*, this freshly unearthed "new Gospel" that would challenge all our understandings of who Jesus was and what he came to do. I got a call from our local NPR affiliate the week it hit bookstores. They wanted to record our Sunday service, since surely I'd be using the time to help people cope with this devastating refutation of our beliefs. When I said I didn't have any plans to bring it up, the reporter was surprised. How could this be avoided?

I asked the reporter if she had noticed how every year—usually right around Easter—the major newsmagazines announced "astounding new information" about who Jesus *really* was? Did that make her suspicious? Was this information truly only discovered at Easter time? And was it noteworthy that those who reported each year's "new" findings had no comment whatsoever about the devastating claims of the previous year? And was it noteworthy that the promoting arm of *The Gospel of Judas* was the National Geographic Society, which had a million-dollar investment in the thing and had gone public with their fears that they couldn't recoup it, short of creating a major media event?

As it turned out, *The Gospel of Judas* was another of many Gnostic Gospels claiming esoteric spiritual insight written (in this case, in Coptic) about two hundred years after the time of Jesus (and the time of the canonical Gospels). It may, of course, have some useful insights to contribute. But it won't contribute anything that's especially *fresh* that the many other Gnostic Gospels haven't gotten to first. And have you heard much about *The Gospel of Judas* recently?

Back to *The Lost Tomb of Jesus*. On the *Today* show, Mr. Cameron said that statisticians argue "in the range of a couple of million to one in favor of [these bones] being [Jesus' and his family's]." And then the next day, the *Boston Globe* printed this: "Amos Kloner, the first archaeologist to examine the site, said the idea fails to hold up by archaeological standards but makes for profitable television. 'They just want to get money for it,' Kloner said."[9]

And the Discovery Channel quietly distanced itself from the whole thing.

Here's a prediction: On your newsstands the week before next Easter, major national newsmagazines will be trumpeting amazing new discoveries about Jesus and his astounding claim to being the resurrected Son of God.

Perhaps one of them will actually turn out to be the real deal. But it seems fair to say that all of them will be reminders that Jesus continues to be really, really interesting.

Three Cheers
for Thoughtful
Atheism!

THERE ARE, OF COURSE, thoughtful alternatives to this adventurous world I've been describing. For instance, as I've noted, we are in a golden age of atheists going public. (Not the first such golden age, by the way, but the first in quite a while.) A few years ago, one prominent yay-for-atheism book was on the market (Sam Harris's *The End of Faith*). Today, a quick scan of my local bookstore picks up maybe a dozen such books. We might wonder if the religious tone of the George W. Bush administration and our conflict with factions of Islam have contributed to this.

Atheists who publish have a leg up on those of us now writing from the God point of view: They're all seriously smart. They tend to have PhDs. But as someone who cut my teeth on great atheists, I can wonder if, for all the brain-power represented among these writers, we've yet to find our Denis Diderot or David Hume or our even our Bertrand Russell or Karl Marx.

Instead, I wonder if we've found our Ann Coulters, Rush Limbaughs, and Al Frankens: provocateurs who are unafraid to play dirty, aren't so good at listening, and—like my local professor who charges praying people with immorality—take delight in provocative but unhelpful accusations.

Despite the recent popularity of these books, many presumably sympathetic people are starting to voice similar concerns. (As per, for one, the *Harper's* review of Richard Dawkins's mega seller *The God Delusion*, which they call "hysterical scientism."[10])

But this hasn't always been so. When I was growing up, my North Star atheist was George Bernard Shaw, and he seems instructive in this current conversation. For one, he actually knew and did his best to care for poor and suffering people. Not for a few years when he was young, but as a lifetime pursuit. These folks weren't just concepts to him, but actual people with faces.

Shaw was also a great artist, which seems wonderful and noteworthy, since wonder itself—the mainspring of most great art—isn't on the table for many atheists. Somehow Shaw got past that (though one might ask if, in the end, he overrelied on polemics and underrelied on emotion, another occupational hazard of atheism, but still). And maybe most astoundingly, Shaw was close friends with and a resolute supporter of his main theistic antagonist, G. K. Chesterton. It seems unthinkable that our current combatants on either side could befriend, listen to, and respect someone with an antithetical point of view.

So in this world where the conversation between secularism and faith is such an important one (read, for instance, the first chapter of *The End of Faith*—Harris says what, at that point at least, no one had said so directly, and good for him), I say three cheers for thoughtful atheism, which did such a service during the Louis XIV era in moving us past theocratic bigotry, warfare, and suppression of thought (hip, hip, hooray for Baruch Spinoza and Ben Franklin and Gotthold Lessing and Voltaire!) and brought us such profoundly helpful things as modern scientific advancement and made a few key contributions to, say, the U.S. Constitution. I like those things! (Whatever the downsides of modern atheism.)

I wonder if Peck's stage theory has anything useful to say here. Perhaps these atheist writers—old and new—are fulfilling the function of stage 3, the "rebellious" stage that presses people in "rules-bound" stage 2 to justify themselves rather than unthinkingly following and promoting pointless, unjustified, and often damaging rules.

This seems powerful as we consider, say, the French Enlightenment. By all accounts, Louis XIV was a stage 1 ("criminal") thug who did some things remarkably well for his purposes. Most notably, he entirely co-opted France's stage 2 religious leaders. He presented himself as their chief supporter, and he proved his point by persecuting their religious enemies.

So the great majority of people of faith who might otherwise have been the most intractable opponents of Louis were neutralized. And what rose up in their place were stage 3 dissidents doing their most central task of unrelentingly shouting that the emperor had no clothes, of using all their "rebellious" energy to—at great personal cost, in that case—dismantle the unholy corruption of stage 2 by stage 1. They *had* to rise up. This was their moment. And the Western world has benefited ever since.

You could argue that something similar happened in Hitler's Germany, except in that case the most noteworthy dissidents came from stage 4 (the "mystical" stage)—Dietrich Bonhoeffer and Martin Niemöller, to name two.

From my point of view, this dialogue was God-ordained, whether it came from atheists or not. Again, these moments had to happen or all was lost, at least for the people and nations in question. And maybe something equally needed will prove to be what's happening now, for all my occasional annoyance with the writers of the moment.

But it seems to me that, as crucial as this back-and-forth is, there's a yearning in the heart of all folks who are resolutely in stage 3 to the effect that there has to be more to life than mocking, taunting, and arguing against the abuses of stage 2. There has to be more than knowing what we're against. For all the rush of this sort of defiance (fair or unfair, worthy or slimy), it historically produces a lot of misery among its proponents. There has to be a stage 4.

I Certainly Need
All the Help
I Can Get

**I'M FINDING MYSELF MISSING OUR NAPKIN
STORIES.** So if you'll indulge me, here are a few more.

I prayed that God would get us out of exhaustive credit card debt from school and emergency medical bills. We made the last payment in about six months, despite both of us being out of work at times and a near-death medical emergency. It was a miracle.

God has freed me from anger, bitterness, and depression.

I was seeking the answers to a very painful experience in my life. Suddenly I realized that I wasn't really seeking a conceptual resolution but a person: God. God has given me comfort and hope in a way I never thought possible.

Here's a thought that's so wild it can either be the worst kind of empty sentimentality or the untrumpable answer. What if what the world needs now—and what you and I need now in our desperate search for a happy day—is primarily this: *God* and *more God*? What if our search for happiness will always be circumscribed and partial? What if our philosophical understandings and plans for world peace, while crucial, will always show their cracks sooner rather than later? And what if our search for God will only take us to good places?

Let's look at another counterproposal for a minute and see where it leads. I'm told that the self-help industry in the United States brings in a cool 8 billion dollars a year—which suggests a next book for me even as I write those words.

And I can see the draw! I love self-help books so much that my love for them wasn't even tarnished by the one self-help seminar I actually went to.

About twenty friends and I spent a day with a leadership and personal empowerment guru who was promoting his two dozen steps to personal and professional success. We had all read the book and liked it just fine, but we knew that there must be additional depth to this material. We held on to this belief right up until the end of his presentation when he told us that to *really* understand the point he had just talked about, we would need to buy the two-hundred-dollar CD set in the lobby. None of us were math whizzes, but multiplied by each of the two dozen steps, that seemed like quite a bit of cash. And technically speaking, we had each already bought his hardback book on the subject and paid the not-insignificant seminar fee. At what point would he actually tell us his points?

Americans want better lives! We're rich, but we don't feel rich. According to the rest of the world's standards we're empowered, but we still feel like victims. As Gregg Easterbrook tells us in his potent book, *The Progress Paradox: How Life Gets Better while People Feel Worse*, every single generation of Americans since our founding has been better off in every measurable way than every preceding generation (crime, real wealth, the likelihood of fighting a war, longevity, work hours). Yet surveys still tell us that we're not getting any happier. Enter self-help, a uniquely American phenomenon.

Self-help has its feet in a number of different pools— spirituality (of course), business, psychology, even sports. Its fundamental insight is straight out of Emerson: Life boils down to self-reliance! Don't play the victim! Quit your excuses! Take charge of your life! Self-help asks us to establish goals and set up measurable steps to reach those goals. It requires a positive attitude. Ideally you'll find a team of life coaches to help you in your journey. And you'll need to take charge of your relationships. If this guy is bad for you, quit playing the victim and act! If this woman is good for you, then set your face like flint toward building the nurturing, lasting relationship you both deserve to have. No one is responsible for your life but you. *You!*

I eat this stuff up. It's like having the greatest-ever high school basketball coach continually yelling at you, calling you only by your last name, telling you to get it in gear. And who among us doesn't need that?

Still, a growing number of folks offer a dissenting viewpoint: The only real downside of self-help is that it doesn't work.

Some of those dissenters are loud and insistent. Steve Salerno, for instance, formerly an editor at one of the leading self-help magazines, *Men's Health*, recently published *SHAM: How the Self-Help Movement Made America Helpless*. He has nothing good to say about any of the self-help superstars and much that's damning, but his fundamental point is that the economic engine of self-help is repeat business. The guru in question tells us some provocative things along the lines I've just outlined and then says that to *really* benefit from the insight, we'll need to buy the superexpensive next step. Salerno paints self-help as the ultimate mirage—tantalizing and always just over the next horizon, a horizon we're told we can get to for only a small additional fee.

I wonder if this is an on-target metaphor for our general search to be happy. Are there helpful things we can do? Absolutely! But those things always seem partial—worthy and powerful on their own terms, but never enough to actually get us across the ever-receding goal line. Did the Enlightenment simultaneously help us and steer us wrong on just this crucial point? Is the "pursuit of happiness" the mother of false leads?

As challenging as a lasting connection to God can be to establish, Jesus promises that if we seek we will find. There is an end to our journey, a country to discover.

And you paid good money for this book. So (stalling while I put together my five-hundred-dollar per session, fifteen-session follow-up) here's my best shot at drawing all the threads together into a rope you can hold on to during your journey there.

PART IV

WELCOME TO YOUR CENTERED-SET LIFE

Some Inside Dirt on Pastors

LET ME TAKE YOU BEHIND THE CURTAIN of many a pastor's life. Those in my line of work often lament the fact that, with all good intentions, we've managed to set up a place where people can enjoy being "in" something—our church, our faith tradition, heaven, something—without it particularly changing their choices or even their experience of life. This, we bemoan, is a far cry from the vibrant life we see among people pursuing the hero's journey in the New Testament. To a one, those people were on pathways with real stakes, real risks, and real rewards. Does the life of the average church person—even someone who's taking us seriously—look *anything* like this? (I'm not going to address whether our *own* lives look anything like this. We're not talking about us right now, thank you very much.)

Even if we concede a dramatically lowered bar, things still look bleak. What percentage of attendees do anything in particular even in their own churches—work the coffee bar, lead a group, help folks get their cars parked, whatever? The standard response from most pastors I know: I can't say for sure, but not many. Leading to: What on earth are we *doing* with our lives? I could have been an architect, just like Dad wanted, but somehow I got suckered into *this*? Excuse me for a moment: I need to go sob quietly in the back room.

I absolutely have moments when I go down that path, but, even so, more often than not I feel cheery as I look at my own winsome, flawed bunch. And the reason boils down to two words: *centered set.*

Or to use another grid we've already looked at: final participation—which, in case it escaped your notice, does include the word *participation.* We have a role in this world, along with a relationship to it. It was that middle (non-participatory) stage that encouraged us to become dispassionate observers of the universe.

In our modern scientific era, we *watch* things—yes, the movement of the planets and the movement of subatomic particles, but also television and movies and sporting events and great church services (presuming you concede such a thing to be possible). But if Owen Barfield is on to something with his stages of participation, we're entering a time when our destiny is tied into *joining in.* We're not the studious wallflowers anymore; now we're the break-dancers.

Which—what do you know?—relates to living in a centered-set world. You'll recall that in a centered set, the issue is whether we're *moving* toward the center dot. In a bounded set, the issue is whether we're inside or outside, which is *static*. In the bounded-set world, once we're inside, we can feel free to pull up an ottoman, grab a drink, and check out what's on cable.

Each of my napkin stories involves people giving faith a try in some fashion and getting back a strikingly good response. Other stories we've talked about involve folks listening to this communicative God and doing what he said—which usually involves something destabilizing that turns out to be powerful. People find themselves moving to Manhattan or Mozambique or the Middle East. People—sometimes me—find themselves risking money or solitude or safety.

Jesus nudges us in this direction. Early in Mark's Gospel, he says the proper response to what he's saying is to "repent" and "believe." And then, just a few words later, Mark gives us a vivid illustration of Jesus' point by introducing four fishermen who meet Jesus and then leave their jobs and families to follow Jesus into a then-unknown adventure. It's as if those two verbs—*leave* and *follow*—are the fleshing out of the two verbs he'd started with: *repent* and *believe*.

Our friend Dietrich Bonhoeffer is all over this, saying:

> If we would follow Jesus we must take certain definite steps. The first step . . . cuts the disciple off from [his or her] previous existence. . . . If [people] imagine that they can follow Jesus without taking this step, they are deluding themselves like fanatics.[11]

And suddenly—what do you know?—all our grids start to tie together. Because now this sounds suspiciously like stage 4, where we're no longer people who simply *believe* the right things but have instead become people embarking on a mystical quest through the uncharted land of stage 4 truth that's bigger than we are. We've stepped out of our ordinary world into the special world. It's hard to over-emphasize this.

I think of a friend I'll call Sue. Sue was a successful advertising executive in San Francisco who suffered from significant depression. But then she had an encounter with God—specifically, an encounter with Jesus. As she experienced this speaking, guiding God, Sue felt that he was encouraging her to take a radical step. She sold her agency and used the money to move to the Haight-Ashbury district, where she hoped to make a real difference for the hundreds of modern-day hippie kids who lived on the streets there.

Other friends joined Sue in those early days, facing all sorts of hardships as they figured out what they were doing. But before long the group began connecting with dozens of kids in a way that made a radical difference. They got calls from grateful parents and became long-term friends with the kids they worked with. Some of these kids, in fact, began to get their own marching orders from this newfound, communicative God. And soon enough some were traveling around the world to wherever other hippie kids (or, as our friends are now calling them, nomadic youth) were. Someone invited Sue to talk on TV about what they were up to, and a woman called in to donate her sprawling Marin County ranch to Sue and her gang so the kids could get away from the city streets for a while. I think I'm fair in saying that Sue had no idea what she'd be getting into when, in her moment of crisis, she asked if there was a God who would take her life somewhere good.

The fundamental question people face when they encounter God is this: Is God an intriguing, profound *concept*? Or is this a God who skews more toward an *experience*, a *relationship*—a God who's eager to guide and empower us if we'll let him? That last question, while achingly enticing, holds a profound threat: If we really pursue that thought, will God take us someplace destabilizing? And as you've picked up, the answer is most certainly yes. But the road to that destabilization is paved with everything we've wanted in life: love, connection, answered prayer, and encouragement that we're in good hands.

We get a lot of tips about how to set off on this destabilizing road most profitably, and unsurprisingly they all encourage the kind of connection and intimacy that's right at the heart of God and this universe he set up.

So Sue, for instance, gathered a team of friends as she began her journey. Grace and I entered into our adventure in Boston with six others. In my quarter century or so of trying to follow God, the majority of that time I've met weekly with a small group of like-minded friends for prayer, encouragement, and support. (These groups tend to turn over every year or two.) We're encouraged not to try life with God alone if at all possible but to constantly pursue this with a team. Remember, alienation is at the heart of all that's bad.

And again, on this faith journey, generosity is encouraged, maybe even mandated. Jesus tells us that the rival god to his Father is, of all things, money. (Directly stated: "You can't worship God and Money.") And his key advice in winning that spiritual battle is overflowing generosity. Generosity *forces* destabilization—how will we ever have enough if we keep giving so much away?—but it also quickly seems to propel us into a living, abundant world like nothing else. I know countless people who give away crazy amounts of money each year, 20 percent of their income or more. (I'm told that by midlife, C. S. Lewis gave away 95 percent of his income. R. G. LeTourneau, a magnate in the earthmoving business, was said to give away 90 percent of his income by the end of his life, and he still died a multimillionaire. And among big-name spiritual leaders of our day, I'm told that Rick and Kay Warren are right there in that neighborhood as well.)

We're encouraged to stay as close to God as possible as we go—to cast all our anxiety on Jesus, as if, when we do, he'll take it. And we'll need to do that, because the nature of this destabilizing journey—following a God who is very much on the move to unknown places—will lead us into uncertainty and eddies and missteps and hardships. On such a journey, we need an actual connection to this God or we'll be crushed and forced to limp back to our starting point.

My Manhattan friends did lose all their money. My Mozambique friends did burn out before the good stuff came. This road with God is about as far from a straight line as imaginable, and this can lead to tumultuous emotions. The antidote we're offered to stress and worrying is prayer and more prayer—constant communication that needs to go both ways.

And we're encouraged to pray for and care for as many *other* people as possible as we go. Sometimes they get helped or encouraged, which makes our own journeys a lot cheerier and also frees us from the inherent narcissism we all tend to lapse into when life seems out of control.

In this world, we note when we're complaining a bit more than we'd like and we tone it down, recognizing that complaining can addict us as quickly as heroin.

And we're helped by great models like Francis—famed for his joy—or Patrick or anyone you know whose faith has taken them not to judgment and strong convictions but to real freedom, encouragement, graciousness, and passionate risk.

I dare you. I'll wager you know people living just this way who would be worth the price of a dinner if you could pump them for insights. Or, alternatively, land a job like mine and get the chance to do exactly that every day, every week, every year.

Where does this leave folks who actually *take* these sorts of destabilizing steps? By definition, these folks feel as though they're living closer to the edge than they wish they were. They usually feel a tremendous need for God to prove yet again that he's actually alive and gives a rip about them and does answer prayer. And yet these are the most passionate, joyful people I know.

These sorts of folks, I suppose, provide another look behind the curtain of a pastor's life. And befriending and going through life with this gang turns out to be the kind of fun you couldn't have imagined possible. Upon further review, maybe you actually *don't* want to be an architect, for all its allures.

If I'd Known This Was Possible, I'd Have Signed Up a Long Time Ago

I'M NOT A GOOD PERSON.

There—I've said it, and I'm glad!

This is new for me, and it still feels uncomfortable because I certainly *hope* to be a good person. I'm not a slacker! I'm doing my best! As an atheist, I would have punched you in the face (or, more likely, *thought* about punching you in the face) if you had suggested I wasn't the best of people (which has to say something ironic). But maybe this explains why Nick Hornby took on such an impossible task with humanizing his leads in *How to Be Good*. We all shy away from people who pay attention to their goodness—or lack thereof—as if, living as we do in a relational universe, being good is a maladaptive strategy for a happy life.

Being a "good person" is fundamentally *defensive*. We bring up our goodness—even if only in our own thoughts—

in order to prove that no one can lay any charges at our feet. It's not a move toward connection; it's a move toward justification.

Let's return for a moment to my atheist writer friends. A good deal of their argument is that people of faith can't reasonably claim that their holy books guide them into being more moral than anyone else. Not to mention that if you actually *read* these books, do you notice what the authors actually put in there? Genocide! Murder! Misogyny! And . . . indeed. You win. While conceding my best effort, I'm not digging in my heels that I'm more moral than anyone else. And yes, the Bible is remarkably candid (which to me is a selling point, but that's something to be argued another day). But in my own defense, like you and everyone on earth, I don't find any particular *hunger* to be more "good" but rather to be more joyful, purposeful, connected.

And having missed out on goodness, I also seem to have missed out on rightness. As I briefly touched on earlier, I've become less interested in "objective truth," if only because it seems to me that the only person who could claim such a thing is God. In the last few centuries, we've done our best to make reason a so-so stand-in for God. But as helpful as it is, reason has proven to get us only so far because we nonetheless start from a limited vantage point. So we're living in a time of newfound interest in *subjective* truth, of truth as we—fallible humans that we are—experience it. Some people see this renewed interest as a natural consequence of stage 4.

It's stage 2, remember, that treats capital-T Truth
as something we can master, get outside of, hold in our
hands, and survey from all angles until it's both tamed and
uninteresting. Stage 4 has happily given up that quest on the
road through its vast country of Truth, all the while recognizing that it can see only as far as the next hill.

The wisdom tradition comes from this perspective.
When we look to sages, we're looking to people who have
walked somewhere that's attractive to us. Now they might
also be the smartest people in the room. They might read
all the best newspapers and they might have thought deeply
about the issues of our day. But in this fundamental area—
the path to a life we'd like to live—they're not primarily
relying on their heads. They don't care if you think of them
as good, and neither do you, as if this is a category mistake.
You simply care about whether they're on to something.

I was foolish about all this in my young adult atheist
days. My persistent arguing with people of faith left me well
respected but not loved—a painful, lonely place to be.

I remember one key moment on, of all places, a golf
course. I was a mediocre player on a good high school golf
team. The team carried a dozen players but only played six,
and I was right on the cusp between sixth and seventh.

I faced another guy on an eighteen-hole play-off for
the coveted sixth spot. Coming into seventeen, we were
tied and I was facing maybe a fifty-foot putt for eagle. If by
some miracle I could sink it, I could pretty much assure
myself the sixth spot. Suddenly the thought that maybe

there was in fact a God seemed pressing. As I lined up the putt, I prayed for the first time since I'd been perhaps seven: *God, if by some chance you're real, if you could help me sink this putt, I'll go to church this Sunday and give you a chance.* I sank the putt—there were a good three breaks to it—and got the sixth spot.

As I packed up my clubs in the parking lot, I remembered the prayer and the bargain I had struck. But I figured that whatever leverage God might have had was now gone. I did, after all, already have what I wanted. As I drove away, I remember thinking, *Sucker. I'm not going to church this week.*

You could make a case that God got the last laugh on that one.

These days I look back on such incidents and shake my head at this God who was so eager to be there the instant I gave him the slightest chance—even under such ridiculous terms by a scoffing little punk. I marvel at the hint of final participation I got that day, in which skepticism could shake hands with a living, vibrant universe.

And let's not kid ourselves. From that edgy, skeptical place, only a few years removed from my bearded, depressed self, I have indeed been knocked into Oz, trivial problems be hanged. While it requires a bold journey to access, there actually seems to be a mind-blowing hidden world available to us all. Since I began this short chapter, (a) a new friend of mine who didn't believe in God's direct work has had a horribly painful, messed-up elbow completely healed after prayer (triggered by a stranger saying to him, "I'm thinking God would like to heal you if your left elbow is messed up"), (b) I've taken some disappointing reversals to God and have since been entirely encouraged, and (c) I've heard several other stunningly encouraging stories (cysts and tumors shrinking after prayer, doctors amazed, etc.).

And even with my complement of problems, it's heartening to realize that they're a different and preferable set than those I once had. There is no amount of money you could pay me to trade that set back.

I think back to a friend who, when challenged that his experience with a responsive and active God was nothing more than a crutch, paused and then replied, "No, I reject that. I'm not sure 'crutch' can fully capture it. To me he's more like an iron lung."

Notes

[1] Owen Barfield, *Saving the Appearances: A Study in Idolatry*, 2nd ed. (Hanover, NH: Wesleyan University Press, 1988).

[2] Tania Ralli, "A Church Takes Root in Unlikely Lefty Soil," *Boston Globe*, December 4, 2005.

[3] G. K. Chesterton, *Orthodoxy* (New York: Image, 2001), 158–59.

[4] Thomas Cahill, *How the Irish Saved Civilization: The Untold Story of Ireland's Heroic Role from the Fall of Rome to the Rise of Medieval Europe* (New York: Doubleday, 1995).

[5] If you want to find out more of their story, check out www.irismin.org.

[6] Dietrich Bonhoeffer, *The Cost of Discipleship* (New York: Macmillan, 1963), 62–63.

[7] James F. Kraus, "The Midlife Happiness Crisis," *Boston Globe*, March 26, 2007, http://www.boston.com/business/globe/articles/2007/03/26/the_midlife_happiness_crisis/; or find the original study at http://www.slate.com/id/2161925/.

[8] "Memoir of Jonathan Edwards," from *The Works of Jonathan Edwards*, volume 1 (Edinburgh: The Banner of Truth Trust, 1974), xxi, emphasis added.

[9] "Filmmaker Claims to Find Jesus' 'Lost Tomb,'" *Boston Globe*, February 27, 2007, D11.

[10] http://www.harpers.org/archive/2006/11/0081282.

[11] Bonhoeffer, *The Cost of Discipleship*, 64–66.

Acknowledgments

A Catholic teacher I like starts each of his teachings with a prayer that his own prejudices won't get in the way. I'm reminded of his prayer as I finish up this book, because so much of the revision process has entailed having prejudice after prejudice pointed out. After my emphatic plea against judgment, was I perhaps judging someone in this or that spot of the manuscript? And indeed. So I was.

All to say, thanks to God for folks willing to take a look at this along the way and help me get out of my own way, insofar as I've been able to. One especially helpful reader was Nancy Hess, who was given the manuscript by one of Tyndale's editors, Jan Long Harris (herself a major shaper of the book along the way). Nancy kindly gave her unvarnished perspective and highlighted more of these dicey areas than I had yet seen.

Brian Housman, Trish Ryan, David Linhart, Amy Thaggard, Andrew and Val Snekvik, my wife Grace, and many others made comments that brought about changes to the book. Thanks also to Lisa Jackson at Tyndale for her detailed edit. Chris Park and Chip MacGregor were super-helpful sounding boards along the way. And back to Jan Long Harris: Showing the key role of God in so much of our lives, Jan was the only nonstudent in the room at a talk I gave to a Tufts University group that was split fairly evenly between students of faith and students from the campus atheist club. She introduced herself after the meeting and suggested there might be a book in the things I'd said. You can be the judge of whether she was on to something.

Just about anything of interest here was first thought of and written about by someone else. I've cited lots of those folks in the book itself, but I've missed some key people like Daniel P. Fuller and Greg Read, who shepherded me into key elements here, and Dutch Sheets and Randy Clark and Brother Lawrence, whose insights show up here.

And most of this book has been shaped by my quirky journey of faith itself, which has taught its own lessons. Some key shapers of that journey—along with Grace—have been Charles Park and Rich and Lisa Lamb, who came up with the idea of this church I'm a part of, which has so transformed my life. Countless people within that community have influenced me and whatever's written here.

About the Author

DAVE SCHMELZER is a playwright and novelist who also pastors the multisite Vineyard Christian Fellowship, Greater Boston. He lives outside of Boston, Massachusetts, with his wife, Grace, and their children.

Do you love to read?

Do you want to go deeper?

Are you in a book group?

ChristianBookGuides.com

Visit today and receive free discussion guides for this book and many other popular titles!

BONUS!

Sign up for the online newsletter and receive the latest news on exciting new books.

CP0070